This book is respectfully dedicated to all who have been persecuted in their quest for Illumination and Transcendence.

OPENING PRAYER

As Masons, we are taught never to commence any great or important undertaking without first invoking the blessing of Deity. I will therefore begin this undertaking with a portion of a prayer excerpted from the Holy Royal Arch degree as the same appears in the American York Rite.

> *"Give us grace diligently to search thy word in the book of nature, wherein the duties of our high vocation are inculcated with Divine authority."*

ALCHEMICALLY STONED

THE PSYCHEDELIC SECRET OF FREEMASONRY

By

P.D. Newman, 32º

The Laudable Pursuit Press

Published by The Laudable Pursuit Press.
2017

The Laudable Pursuit

Copyright © 2017 by The Laudable Pursuit Press

Edited by Jason E. Marshall, 32°

Layout, cover, and back cover by Matthew D. Anthony, 32°

ISBN: 978-0-578-19400-4

The Laudable Pursuit
www.thelaudablepursuit.com
Email: editor@thelaudablepursuit.com

Printed by Lulu.com

TABLE OF CONTENTS

PART I: ACACIA
The Sprig of Acacia and DMT *20*
DMT and the Russian Rite of Melissino *28*
DMT and Count Cagliostro's Egyptian Rite *32*
DMT and the Fratres Lucis *40*
Endogenous DMT Production and the Pineal Gland *42*
DMT Conclusion *46*
Union of the Plants *48*

PART II: ERGOT
Masonry and the Mysteries of Eleusis *54*
Threshing Floors and Waterfalls *62*
The Vine of the Serpent *70*

PART III: FLY AGARIC
Masonic Templary, Guardians of the Grail *76*
Baphoment and the Golden Fleece *80*
The Holy Grail and Soma *86*
The Christian Connection *92*
The Phoenix, the Rose Cross, and the Royal Secret *96*
Mushrooms Among Rosicrucians *100*
Aleister and Amanitas *108*
Pythagoras' Hecatomb *112*
The Hoope-bird and the Shamir Worm *116*
Concluding Remarks *120*

PART IV: SUPPLEMENTAL PAPERS ON PSILOCYBIN MUSHROOMS
Psilocybe Cubensis: A Worth Candidate for the Philosphers's Stone..*126*
Before The Wassons, Part I: Magic Mushrooms in North America....*132*
Before The Wassons, Part II: Magic Mushrooms in the United Kingdom
....*136*
Sukaramaddava and Psilocybin *140*

APPENDIX
Dimethyltryptamine Experience Reports *144*
Further Reading on Entheogens *176*
Further Reading on Freemasonry *178*
Works Cited *180*

Acknowledgements

I would like to mention a number of important people, without whose aid and assistance this book may never have seen the light of day. First and foremost I would like to thank my amazing wife Rebecca Newman for her enduring support and patience during the writing process. You are my cornerstone and my muse. I am grateful also to Chris Bennett, Michael S. Downs, Dr. David Harrison, Steve Burkle, and Arturo de Hoyos. Your friendships and guidance have made a world of difference. I would also like to thank Ryan Whittenburg, Susan and Mike Dye, and an anonymous Master Mason from Rice University for their financial contributions to this project. Finally, I want to thank Jason Marshall, Matt Anthony, and The Laudable Pursuit for making this publication a possibility.

Foreword

In this sensational new book, P.D. Newman argues that the use of DMT was an essential ingredient in certain Masonic Rites, especially Cagliostro's Egyptian Rite and Melissino's Rite, something that added to the overall ritualistic experience. These lost rites of the eighteenth century are something that I'm deeply interested in, and the idea that certain rites included the digestion or smoking of the root extracts of a certain species of acacia that had hallucinogenic properties to produce an effect in a particular 'lodge' room is a fascinating one. Newman's work details the use of DMT in various initiation rituals throughout history and provides an argument for his theory that is at once convincing, entertaining and interesting.

The sprig of acacia is a strong symbol within Freemasonry, and Newman presents us with a new twist on the meaning behind this symbol. Newman also presents us with the history of the acacia symbol within Freemasonry, from its mention in eighteenth century exposes, and how during the third degree, it became an essential ingredient in the Master Mason ritual, perhaps in more ways than one.

- Dr. David Harrison, author of *The Genesis of Freemasonry*

AUTHOR'S PREFACE

Admittedly, I'm a scholastic amateur. My only credential is that I am a member of the Masonic Fraternity. I am, however, uniquely qualified to write this book. Before becoming a Freemason I spent the previous decade and a half studying entheogens and their role in different cultures, religions, indigenous societies, and ancient mystery traditions. Much of that time was also spent experimenting with many of those same entheogenic compounds, provided I could acquire and ingest them safely and without fear of legal repercussions. During said period I had the great fortune to commune with plant sacraments as diverse as ayahuasca, *Salvia divinorum*, sacred cacti, 'magic mushrooms,' so-called Hawaiian baby woodrose seeds, and more – and all on more than one occasion; some on hundreds of occasions. I can say without hesitation and without a doubt that those experiences are counted among the most precious and meaningful of my entire life.

And, that isn't easy to say – not in my culture, at least. Indeed, in most of the West drugs which are deemed to have *no medicinal value* have been demonized and criminalized. There has been no real effort made to distinguish the very substantial differences between plant entheogens on the one hand, and addictive, detrimental compounds such as, say, crack cocaine, crystal methamphetamine, or heroin, on the other. But, there is a difference; a big one. Where crack, meth, and heroin, etc. make of one a slave, held captive and abused by the drug, entheogens have the direct opposite effect. Entheogenic compounds are known to be liberating of the spirit and expanding of the mind and consciousness. They serve to *open the mind*, so to speak, to different and previously unfathomed modes of thought and awareness. The word *entheogen* literally means *that which generates the divine within*. Recent evidence has even shown that, contrary to the fallacious claims touted by the DEA and FDA for the past half a century that entheogenic compounds kill brain cells, etc., some entheogens actually have the ability to *regrow* degenerated brain cells.[1] I think that alone is pretty remarkable. And that is to say nothing of their therapeutic value for those suffering from terminal illnesses, nervous disorders such as PTSD, alcoholism and addiction, and a whole host of other diseases and disorders that are difficult or even impossible to treat or cure.

---

1   Catlow, B.J. *Effects of psilocybin on hippocampal neurogenesis and extinction of trace fear conditioning.*

That having been said, I did not petition for the three degrees of Masonry expecting to find evidence of entheogenic symbolism. On the contrary, following one particularly profound and life-changing entheogenic experience, I made the decision to set aside entheogens for an undetermined amount of time and focus my efforts instead on the attainment of initiation along more traditional avenues; avenues that are socially accepted within my own culture. Those efforts led me to the door of Masonry, where I knocked and the Lodge was opened to me. Once inside, it was both a shock and a pleasant surprise to find evidence of symbolism pointing back to those same entheogenic compounds that had first set me on the path which led me to Freemasonry. I had come full circle, I felt, and this small book is my meager attempt to document those discoveries.

It must also be said that, although entheogenic symbols may very well be present within Masonic ritual, Freemasonry does not condone the use of illegal drugs in any way, shape, or form. We as Free and Accepted Masons are explicitly charged with the task of being peaceful citizens, and cheerfully conforming to the laws of the countries wherein we reside. However, Freemasonry accepts good men of all faiths, provided those men profess a belief in both a supreme being and in the immortality of the soul. There is no shortage of religious organizations in the West, including the Native American Church, *União do Vegetal*, and *Santo Daime*, which adhere to those same beliefs and also happen to be granted the legal right to use certain entheogenic compounds sacramentally so long as those compounds are employed within the ceremonial context of their own religion. Furthermore, not all entheogens are illegal outside of religious use. There are no current laws in the US, for example, against the consumption of plant sacraments such as *Amanita muscaria* mushrooms, *Argyreia nervosa* seeds, the seeds of the various *Ipomoea*, or *Datura stramonium* seeds, etc., all of which have a long history of religious and initiatory use. Therefore, should you choose to experiment with any of the entheogenic compounds discussed in this book, whether you're a Mason or otherwise, I urge you to do so safely and within the confines of the laws of the state or country wherein you reside.

Lastly, do your research. We are instructed in *Mutus Liber*, "*Ore, lege, lege, lege, relege, labora et invenies;*" Pray, read, read, read, read again, and then, l*abor and discover*. Proper identification and preparation and especially correct dosage is paramount. As the Alchemist and physician Paracelsus once warned, poison is in everything, and that which makes of something a poison or a remedy is merely the *dosage*.

Travel *light*.

December 27, 2014
Myrtle, Mississippi

Introduction

Throughout history there have been seemingly spontaneous outbreaks of spirituality, sometimes leading to the later formation of religious cults and institutions. We see it happening today as well, all over the world, at a historically unprecedented pace. New cults, new religions, new messiahs and guru figures are rising up everywhere we look, many or most of them crashing back down to Earth sometime later, leaving believers to pick up the pieces of their lives for themselves..

Such developments can be both positive and negative: positive if the leaders and organizations operate ethically and morally, negative if they do not. Too often we have seen charismatic leaders and movements entice people into giving up their autonomy in service of a guru or group, and often their money and possessions as well. Followers become virtually hypnotized. Sometimes spouses and children are parted and indoctrinated separately, to their ultimate detriment. Sexual favors are often demanded; indeed, sometimes people's very lives are sacrificed. Some guru figures even give powerful drugs to their followers surreptitiously to keep them inline and "believing," as we saw with the followers of Jim Jones.

History also records the many attempts to help keep humanity operating from a place of cooperation and compassion, rather than from competition and greed. Such attempts are often viewed suspiciously or maligned out of hand by those lacking in the very virtues these groups espouse, and these attempts get labeled as evil conspiracies, or as the very type of cult they are trying to protect people from. However, the fact that the "good" groups also have secret rituals to which the non-initiated are not privy arouses the same deep suspicions as do the "bad" groups. Perhaps the most famous of the organizations – and the one most often accused of skullduggery – is the Masonic Order. Yet Masons claim very high moral and ethical ground for themselves.

Well and good, but if everything one's groups does is ethical and beneficial, what is the need for secrecy? This is the big question, and it's one that Masons traditionally have had a hard time answering to the satisfaction of those wanting to know more. But perhaps there is a very good reason for the secrecy. What if the sprig of acacia in the Master Mason degree is more than a symbol? What if the sprig of acacia was originally intended to help the candidate actually experience the deep spiritual and magnanimous nature of his initiatory vows and admonitions – indeed, of his very being? And what if the active compounds of that sprig were deemed "illegal" or "irreligious" or "demonic" by one's society or religion? Might not these seem good reasons for maintaining secrecy?

P.D. Newman, himself a 32nd degree Mason, has been studying this problem from the inside out, and back in again, for many years. He likes evidence, and he knows that evidence is not always in obvious places. He also knows that evidence, even as good as that presented here, is not necessarily proof – but don't let that stop you, dear reader, from seeing it that way.

- Clark Heinrich, author of *Strange Fruit*

PART I: ACACIA

THE SPRIG OF ACACIA AND DMT

"Q. What qualifies a Man for the Seventh Order [of Masonry]?
A. [The] composition of the Grand Elixir." [1]

The sprig of acacia is an important symbol within Freemasonry. But, as you're about to learn, unbeknownst even to the Fraternity's own initiates, the acacia is rich in more than just symbolism. The theory to be here set forth is surely the most controversial that Masonry has seen espoused by one of Her own acolytes since 1912, when Theodor Reuss declared boldly that "[sexual magic is] the KEY which opens up all Masonic and Hermetic secrets."[2] And, at first exposure, one might even suspect that ours is an equally outrageous proposal. Truly, what we propose is just as, if not more, taboo than the notion of sexual magic. For, our solution is a hallucinogenic drug; namely, DMT or *dimethyltryptamine*. The reader is therefore asked to maintain an open – if skeptical – mind.

It is said allegorically that a sprig of acacia marked the head of the grave of our beloved Grand Master Hiram Abiff, leading those travel-weary Fellows of the Craft to discover the location where the three despicable ruffians had deposited his precious remains. In addition to its presence in the Master Mason degree, the sprig of acacia also appears in the Perfect Master degree[3], is mentioned in the Elu of the Nine degree[4], and is depicted on the cordon, as well as being referenced in the degree of Perfect Elu[5] in the Southern Jurisdiction of the Ancient and Accepted Scottish Rite. Symbolically, the sprig of acacia is said to be emblematical of "our faith in the immortality of the soul," and this on account of the fact that the acacia, we are told, is an evergreen.[6] However, perhaps there is still yet something more to this humble yet *potent* symbol. For, as we shall soon see, the acacia and related plants have been an important fixture in many of the ancient Mystery traditions.

---

1   Morris, S. Brent. *The Post Boy Sham Exposure of 1723.*
2   Ford, Gary. *The O.T.O. is Clandestine Masonry.*
3   5th Degree, AASR.
4   9th Degree, AASR.
5   14th Degree, AASR.
6   Depending on the species, acacia can be either deciduous or evergreen. The species of acacia native to Jerusalem which is the prime candidate for the acacia appearing in the Master Mason degree, *Acacia senegal*, is deciduous.

And, in the rites of passage and shamanic ceremonies of some still extant indigenous and semi-civilized societies, they still serve as far more than simply powerful symbols.

In the formidable lecture he penned for the Master Mason degree, Albert Pike wrote in *Morals and Dogma* that the acacia is

> *"the same tree which grew up around the body of Osiris. It was sacred among the Arabs, who made of it the idol Al-Uzza, which Mohammed destroyed. It is abundant as a bush in the Desert of Thur: and of it the 'crown of thorns' was composed, which was set on the forehead of Jesus of Nazareth. It is a fit type of immortality on account of its tenacity of life; for it has been known, when planted as a doorpost, to take root again and shoot out budding boughs over the threshold."* [7]

In an unassuming footnote to the Master Mason degree in his recently issued book Masonic Formulas and Rituals, Pike added that the

> *"branch of Acacia [is] in memory of the true cross, which, it is said, was made of that wood. This branch of Acacia took the place of the branch of myrtle, which the initiates of Memphis bore. ...[T]he bough of gold, which Virgil gives Eneas, wherewith to descend to the infernal regions, has the same origin."* [8]

Finally, in the Perfect Elu degree of the Ancient and Accepted Scottish Rite, Southern Jurisdiction, we learn in the *Legenda* that

> *"the acacia...is that genus of trees to which belong that which yields the gum arabic, the mezquite, and the locust. It is the satah or satam wood of the Hebrew writings, ...used in the construction of the Tabernacle and the Temple, and therefore a Symbol of Holiness and Divine Truth. ...It is...not the Symbol of Immortality alone, but of that life of innocence and purity for which the Faithful hope when they shall have been raised up to a new and spiritual existence."* [9]

In the earliest versions of the Master Mason degree there is no mention made anywhere of a sprig of acacia. Rather, the references are to a sprig

---

[7] De Hoyos, Arturo. *Albert Pike's Morals and Dogma: Annotated Edition.*, P. 155.
[8] De Hoyos, Arturo. *Albert Pike's Masonic Formulas and Rituals*, P. 112.
[9] Pike, Albert. *Legenda of the Lodge of Perfection*, P. 12.

of *cassia*, a different plant altogether possessed of no real psychotropic value. Cassia, botanically labeled Cinnamonum cassia, is a cinnamon-like evergreen originating in southern China[10], whereas acacia, which can be either evergreen or deciduous, is a genus of nearly one thousand species, with all but ten or so of those having their origin in Australia.[11] Sometime between the 1730s and 1745, a change was made across the board, and *cassia* would forever become *acacia* in Masonic ritual. Masonic scholar Albert G. Mackey argued in his *Encyclopedia* that the original inclusion of cassia in the Master Mason degree was but an error that likely arose "from the very common habit among illiterate people of sinking the sound of the letter a in the pronunciation of any word of which it constitutes the initial syllable."[12] *Acacia* would therefore have become *cassia*. However, we are not so convinced. There is absolutely no evidence supporting the supposition that the switch from cassia to acacia was not a deliberate one. Furthermore, even William Preston, who is largely responsible for the degrees *as we have come to know them*, provided cassia in his draft of the Master Mason degree. One would be hard pressed to explain how a man of Preston's caliber and literacy would fail to be able to pronounce a word as mere and common as is *acacia*. While we do not know who is responsible for implementing this change, we may have discovered the reason *why* the switch was made. Our solution is at once Alchemical and entheogenic.

The convergence of Freemasonry with Alchemy goes at least as far back as the early 1720s, when John Theophilus Desaguliers (1683-1744) served as the third Grand Master of the first Grand Lodge in London. Desaguliers acted as research assistant to Sir Isaac Newton in the Royal Society, each of whom are known to have been Alchemically inclined, if not actual practicing Alchemists. In fact, in early 2016 a recipe for the production of the legendary philosopher's stone, taken from Starkey and written in Newton's own hand, was discovered in a private collection.[13] If anyone was indeed behind the widespread switch from cassia to acacia in the Master Mason degree, Desaguliers, powerful in Masonry and knowledgeable in matters of Alchemy, is perhaps the best candidate. After all, he is suspected of having been instrumental in the very development of the Master Mason degree.[14] Moreover, in her book *John Theophilius Desaguliers: A Natural Philosopher, Engineer, and Freemason in Newtonian England*, Audrey T. Carpenter discusses a letter wherein the Duke of Chandos urged Desaguliers to persuade the alchemist Baron Silburghe, who claimed to have been success-

---

10   Li, Xi-Wen. *Cinnamonum Cassia*.
11   Pedley, Les. *Another View of Racosperma*.
12   Mackey, Albert G., "CASSIA" *Encyclopedia of Freemasonry and Its Kindred Sciences*, P. 248.
13   Greshko, Michael. *Isaac Newton's Lost Alchemy Recipe Rediscovered*.
14   Harrison, David. *The Masonic Enlightenment: John Theophilus Desaguliers and the Birth of Modern Freemasonry*.

ful in the transmutation of base metals into gold via quicksilver, into giving up some of his alchemical secrets.[15] At the very least, these associations demonstrate that Desaguliers harbored more than a passing interest in the Royal Art.

The principle goal of the Alchemists was the production of the *lapis philosophorum* or philosopher's stone, the stone of the wise, from the secret *prima materia* or primal matter. As the Alchemical axiom states, the *lapis* is made "not of stone, not of bone, not of metal."[16] That is to say, it comes not from the mineral kingdom and not from the animal kingdom. It must therefore be deduced that this stone is only to be found in the vegetable kingdom; namely, within the acacia, Masonry's prima materia. Many present day Alchemists are content to produce stones from virtually any mineral, metal, plant, or animal, ascribing the value of those stones solely to their attributed planetary signatures. However, for a stone to meet the criteria of the true stone of the wise, imagined planetary signatures will not suffice. It must first satisfy specific requirements, chief among them being the conferral upon its possessor of the gift of immortality.

Let it here be said that the Alchemical vocation is no vain search for physical immortality. Bodily longevity is not the variety of immortality here described. The famous mythologist Joseph Campbell explains rightly that

> *"the search for physical immortality proceeds from a misunderstanding of the traditional teaching. On the contrary, the basic problem is: to enlarge the pupil of the eye, so that the body with its attendant personality will no longer obstruct the view. Immortality is then experienced as a present fact."* [17]

Indeed, the Alchemists purport that the stone of the wise has the power to provide its possessor with the knowledge of his very immortal soul. Hence it also being called the *stone of projection*. For, the soul of its possessor is the very thing that appears to be projected upon the stone's proper application. Liberated from its bodily frame, the stone-projected soul is free to roam the so-called *astral plane*, loosed from the limitations of its corporeal container – a concept that has come to be known as an *out of body experience* or *OBE*.

Conveniently, there exists a special class of truly magical plants that actually satisfies the above listed criteria. We speak here of entheogens. As the word implies, entheogenic plants are those which generate an experience of one's divinity within; that is, entheogens have the potential to facilitate what appears to be the direct experience of one's own immortal soul; of the continuity of consciousness independent of the mortal frame. And, certain species of

---

15   Carpenter, Audrey T. *John Theophilus Desaguliers: A Natural Philosopher, Engineer, and Freemason in Newtonian England*, P. 173.
16   Heinrich, Clark. *Strange Fruit: Alchemy and Religion, the Hidden Truth*, P. 165.
17   Campbell, Joseph. *The Hero with a Thousand Faces*, P. 161.

acacia – a symbol which Masonic ritual plainly tells us is emblematical of "our faith in the immortality of the soul" – naturally constitute a portion of these plant entheogens.

As was explained, Acacia is a genus of nearly one thousand species of tree, some one hundred of which are known to contain concentrated amounts of the powerful psychedelic compound DMT. DMT has been used in a ceremonial context among a number of indigenous groups, most notably the *ayahuasca*-drinking tribes of Amazonia and the *yopo*-snuffing peoples in the Caribbean.

Ayahuasca, also known as *yage*, depending on the dialect, is a ceremonial beverage prepared by combining DMT-containing plants such as *Psychotria viridis* and/or *Diplopterys cabrerana* with the monoamine oxidase inhibitor-containing liana *Banisteriopsis cappi*. For, DMT is not normally orally active due to the presence of monoamine oxidase in the gut. But, when combined with a monoamine oxidase inhibitor (or MAOI), it becomes so.[18] The effects are profoundly psychedelic and last for up to six hours after drinking. Yopo, on the other hand, also known as *epena*, is a ritualistic snuff that is prepared by combining the DMT-rich seeds of *Anadenanthera colubrina* or *Anadenanthera peregrina* with calcium carbonate that has been created from the calcinated shells of crustaceans, thereby rendering the snuff absorbable by the mucous membranes in the nasal cavity.[19] Unlike ayahuasca, the effects of yopo last only a few minutes after each insufflation.

While neither ayahuasca nor yopo are prepared from a species acacia, the latter has certainly been known to have been used in a multitude of entheogenic and inebriating contexts. In Mexico, for example, the roots of *Acacia angustifolia* are added to *pulque*, a fermented beverage prepared from the *agave* cactus. (Ratsch, p. 28) In West Africa, the leaves and bark of *Acacia campylacantha* are added to *dolo*, a brew prepared from sorghum, pennisetum, and honey. Dolo is said to impart strength in its drinker and lift the mood.[20] In India, Indonesia, and Malaysia can be found *Acacia catechu*, from which is concocted a substance used as an additive to *betel quids*. Betal quids are consumed by putting a small amount in the mouth between the gum and cheek, similar to how chewing tobacco is consumed, and depending on the mixture acts as either a stimulant or a sedative. In India, too, are two more species of acacia – *nilotica* and *farnesiana* – from which are prepared traditional aphrodisiacs and muscle relaxants. (Ratsch, p. 29) In South America a brew called *balche* is prepared from the bark

---

18 Metzner, Ralph. *Sacred Vine of Spirits: Ayahuasca*, P. 1.
19 Torres, Constantino Manuel. *Anadenanthera: Visionary Plant of Ancient South America*, P. 53.
20 Ratsch, Christian. *The Encyclopedia of Psychoactive Plants: Ethnopharmacology and Its Applications*, P. 28

of *Acacia cornigera*.[21] And, in Australia a wide variety of acacia leaves are burned as a medicinal smoke. Even here in America, the root bark of a species of acacia, albeit not a psychoactive variety, is a key ingredient in some soft drinks, including the Biloxi, Mississippi-based Barq's Root Beer®.

An important tree within the Hebrew tradition, the Ark of the Covenant is said to have been constructed using acacia wood. Acacia has even been proposed as the source of Moses' various visions recounted in the Volume of the Sacred Law. In his paper *Biblical Entheogens: A Speculative Hypothesis*, Benny Shanon, the Professor of Psychology at Hebrew University in Israel, speculated that a local species of DMT-rich acacia (such as *Acacia senegal*) could have been combined with the native MAOI-containing *Peganum harmala* bush, known also as *Syrian rue*, to produce a psychedelic brew chemically indistinguishable from the Amazonian ayahuasca.[22]

As a side note, *Peganum harmala* is currently employed along with a species of acacia by the Fatimiya Sufi order, where an ayahuasca-like beverage plays a central role in their techniques of ecstasy. According to N. Wahid Azal, the founder of the Fatimiya Sufi order,

> "*[Peganum harmala] has an old and central role in the Mazdean religion of ancient Iran and continues to do so to this very day amongst Iranian Shi'ites, be they Twelver, Isma'ili, or Sufi. The Zoroastrians properly consider it to be the most sacred of their herbs, and in Persian it is known as Esfand… Esfand is a shortened version of the Pahlavi form of the name Esfandmorz who is the Avestan Spendarmat or Spenta Armaiti, (trans. 'Holy' or 'Beneficent Devition') namely, the Zoroastrian Archangel of the Earth who is one of the six Amesha Spenta (trans. 'Bounteous Immortals') or archangelic hypostases of the Godhead Ahura Mazda/ Ohrmazd.*"[23]

The six "Amesha Spenta" of course play a part in the degree of Master of the Royal Secret, the thirty-second degree of the Ancient and Accepted Scottish Rite of Freemasonry.

Attempts to align the origins of Freemasonry with Sufism have been made by a number of researchers, chief among them being Idris Shah and Gerard de Nerval. Hashish enthusiast and member of the cannabis club *Le Club de Haschischinns*, de Nerval, in his tome *Voyage to the Orient*, offered a prequel to the story of Masonic hero Hiram Abiff, claiming to have overheard

---

21   *Ibid* at 29
22   Shanon, Benny. *Biblical Entheogens: A Speculative Hypothesis*.
23   Propaganda Anonymous. *The Fatimiya Sufi Order and Ayahuasca*.

the "folk-tale" while smoking hashish in a café in Constantinople. Sir Richard Frances Bacon, also an enthusiast of hashish, too wrote that "Sufi-ism [is] the Eastern parent of Freemasonry."[24]

We have seen that acacia's psychoactive potential has not been lost on at least one Sufi order. Therefore, if Sufism was indeed one of the contributing influences on Freemasonry, the same may be one more possible explanation for how the acacia found its way into the Craft.

In addition to the plant world, DMT is also produced endogenously; that is, it is manufactured within and by the human body, as well as other living organisms. Although, where in the human body it is produced and under what circumstances still remains a medical mystery[25]. It is believed by some to be responsible for a number of spontaneous spiritual experiences, including mystical visions, out of body, and near death experiences. This makes the compound quite different from the other classic hallucinogens, all of which are to be found only within the vegetable kingdom. But, while far, far more powerful, the effects of DMT are really very similar to those of *mescaline, psilocybin*, and LSD. In the colorful words of the late psychedelic philosopher Terence McKenna,

> "*The experience that engulfs one's entire being as one slips beneath the surface of the DMT ecstasy feels like the penetration of a membrane. The mind and the self literally unfold before one's eyes. There is a sense that one is made new, yet unchanged, as if one were made of gold and had just been recast in the furnace of one's birth. ...Under the influence of DMT the world becomes and Arabian labyrinth, a palace, a more than possible Martian jewel, vast with motifs that flood the gaping mind with complex and wordless awe. Color and the sense of a reality-unlocking secret nearby pervade the experience. There is a sense of other times, and of one's own infancy, and of wonder, wonder, and more wonder. ...Many diminutive beings are present there ...One has the impression of entering into an ecology of souls that lies beyond the portals of what we naively call death. ...Here is a tremendum barely to be told, an epiphany beyond our wildest dreams. Here is the realm of that which is stranger than we can suppose. Here is the mystery, alive, unscathed, still as new for us as when our ancestors lived it fifteen thousand summers ago. ...The sense of emotional connection is*

---

24   Bennett, Chris. *Cannabis: The Philosopher's Stone.*
25   On May 23, 2013 Cottonwood Research Foundation Inc. announced that DMT had officially been discovered in the pineal glands of live rats. (Cottonwood Research Foundation Inc.)

terrifying and intense. The Mysteries revealed are real and if ever fully told will leave no stone upon another in the small world we have gone so ill in." [26]

Truly, the DMT experience is the very stuff of religious or spiritual ecstasy. It is no wonder then that certain Alchemically-inclined Freemasons who were privy to its psychedelic secret chose to interpret and employ the acacia in a similar light.

These claims should come as no surprise considering the fact that DMT is one of the most powerful psychoactive compounds known to science. It is a substance which has been used by indigenous people for centuries to induce an experience that has been subjectively interpreted, time and time again, as the very liberation of the immortal soul from the gross, physical body, thereby permitting it to wander freely the spiritual planes of existential reality; however, unfortunately, it is now relegated to the list of scheduled narcotics under the Controlled Substances Act.[27]

Still, not every culture shares the West's conservative sentiments regarding naturally-growing visionary compounds. According to Benny Shanon, the professor of psychology at the Hebrew University of Jerusalem in Israel,

"[t]he recourse of powerful psychoactive plants and preparations in order to establish contact with the higher realms of spirituality has been at the very heart of shamanic practices all over the globe." [28]

Whether we're talking about the *soma* of the Vedas, the *haoma* of the Zoroastrians, or the mysterious *kykeon* of the Eleusinian Mysteries, there is no debating that entheogenic compounds have played a vital role in the development of a number of religious doctrines and practices around the world. Therefore, these sacred compounds have played a prominent role in the lives of a multitude of worshippers. And, while these ancient rites are in most cases no longer enacted in the same extreme way which they once were, in many instances the symbols of these entheogens still persist, not unlike the sprig of acacia in Freemasonry. These somewhat hidden, yet still powerful, symbols communicate powerful truths to those that have the eyes to see and ears to listen.

---

26   McKenna, Terence. *Food of the Gods*. P. 257-258.
27   DMT is currently listed as a Schedule I, which means that according to the government, it has no currently accepted medical use, even under medical supervision, and that it has at least some potential for abuse.
28   Shanon

DMT AND THE RUSSIAN RITE OF MELISSINO

"Now...we shall see...why David said: regnavit a ligno Deus[1]."
- Melissino[2]

The first author to our knowledge to actually offer an entheogenic solution for the problem of the acacia symbol in Freemasonry was Carl A.P. Ruck, the Professor of Classics at Boston University in Massachusetts, who wrote in his book *Mushrooms, Myth and Mithras: The Drug Cult That Civilized Europe*:

> "The murdered body of Hiram Abiff, a Master Mason and Master of Works on Solomon's Temple, was 'raised' from his resting place beneath an acacia sprig which marked the spot to those who would be sent by King Solomon to search. After the interred corpse of Hiram was found, Solomon himself went to the site to recover the body. Feeling beneath the ground at the site of the acacia, the king felt Hiram's 'hand.' In the process of recovering his corpse, he first used the grip of the Entered Apprentice, then that of the Fellowcraft, but twice felt the skin slipping off Hiram's hand. Finally Solomon used the grip of a Master Mason to raise the corpse. In the entheobotanical context, we feel that this myth is a description of a ritualized acacia harvest. We note that the subterranean root bark of acacia...species are known to contain high levels of Dimethyltryptamine, an entheogen which is strongly psychoactive when extracted." [3]

Little did the professor know, there exist actual examples of

---
1 "God reigns from a tree."
2 De Hoyos, Arturo. *The Melissino System of Freemasonry*, P. 92.
3 Ruck, Carl A.P. *Mushrooms, Myth and Mithras: The Drug Cult that Civilized Europe*, P. 225.

acacia-produced DMT and its use in 18th century Masonic ritual.

The earliest known Freemason to allude to the production of DMT from acacia was Alchemist and General of the Artillery of the Russian Empire Pyotr Ivanovich Melissino, widely considered to be the greatest Russian artilleryman of the 18th century. In 1762 Melissino established a theurgic, Alchemico-Masonic rite which drew heavily upon mystic Christian themes. We must credit Arturo de Hoyos, the Grand Archivist and Grand Historian of the Southern Jurisdiction of the Ancient and Accepted Scottish Rite, with the discovery of the following quotation. Illustrious Brother De Hoyos was gracious enough to contact us after translating the Melissino rite, suggesting that we include the following excerpt in our manuscript.

In the seventh degree of his rite, Melissino specifically refers to the acacia as the primal matter of the Alchemists, from which is produced a stone – DMT salt crystals, a veritable vegetable stone – the same being identified as the legendary stone of the philosophers. Melissino says that

> *"The cubical stone is the alkaline universal-salt ... The Master's Degree speaks to us of the acacia found upon Hiram's grave. This is the true [primal] matter, from which the philosophers create their treasures. It is the true light of the world, from which glorious Hiram shall rise again under the guise of the Redeemer. It is the burning coal of which Isaiah (in chap. 6:6-7) [speaks], and which must be prepared in accordance with the secret system of the wise men of old and the philosophers [i.e., the Alchemists].*
>
> *One of our most mysterious materials is therefore the burning coal, which the Egyptian Kabbalah names clearly and without fuss."* [4]

What other than DMT could the "treasures" created from acacia have been? Of course, "cubical stone" is language which Melissino has obviously borrowed from Masonic ritual, which refers to the perfect ashlar, but here he has clearly identified this ashlar with a "salt" that has been Alchemically produced from acacia. And indeed, DMT is just that. It's not a base. It's a salt. The scriptural allusion in the above excerpt refers to a biblical episode wherein a burning coal of an unspecified

---
4   De Hoyos, *Melissino*, P. 88-89.

substance is placed upon Isaiah's lips by an angel, assumedly for him to inhale its fumes; that is, for him to *smoke* it – smoking being one of the preferred modes by which DMT is normally consumed. "Lo" said the angel. "This [burning coal] hath touched thy lips; and thine iniquity is taken away, and thy sin is purged."[5] Note that *acacia* or *akakia*, as Mackey related it in his *Lexicon*, is suggestive of *freedom from iniquity* or *freedom from sin*.[6] "Thine iniquity is taken away, and thy sin is purged," indeed. One wonders how far back this tradition actually stretches.

Whatever the case, it is quite apparent that Melissino knew something very special about the acacia. Moreover, Melissino was not the only Russian mystic to have preoccupied himself with treasures extracted from a tree. According to G.I. Gurdjieff's biographer James Webb, the founder of the *Fourth Way* once claimed cryptically that

> *"only three drugs from the whole Western pharmacopeia were useful -- opium, castor oil and an unidentified substance extracted from a certain tree."* [7]

As Gurdjieff's teachings were derived in part from a form of Freemasonry, it is not impossible that Gurdjieff's "unidentified substance" and "certain tree" are none other than DMT and a species of acacia, respectively, and that he learned of the secret from a fellow Russian who was knowledgeable not only of Melissino and his rite but also of chemistry. We can only speculate.

---

5   *The Holy Bible, KJV*, Isa. 6
6   Mackey, Albert G. *A Lexicon of Freemasonry*, P. 4.
7   L.I.G.H.T. *Drugs, Alcohol and Food.*

DMT AND COUNT CAGLIOSTRO'S EGYPTIAN RITE

Nearly two decades after the establishment of Melissino's rite in Russia, London saw the appearance of another theurgic, Alchemico-Masonic rite which also employed the acacia in an entheogenic context: Count Alessandro di Cagliostro's Egyptian Rite of Freemasonry. A close friend and colleague of Melissino, Cagliostro was an Italian Alchemist, healer, and magician who died while unfairly imprisoned for the crime of heresy.

The parallels between Cagliostro's use of the acacia and that of Melissino are readily apparent. In the Apprentice and Companion lectures of his Egyptian Rite, the acacia is again referred to as being the primal matter in a very specific Alchemical operation. When properly executed, this operation results in the production of a "cubical ashlar;" that is, the result is a purified, crystalline stone or salt that has been produced from the acacia. This stone is then dissolved into a "red liqueur," which is afterward imbibed by the candidate for initiation. Cagliostro's ritual states:

> "*The acacia is the primal matter and [when] the rough ashlar or mercurial part has been purified, it becomes cubical...It is thus that you may bring about the marriage of the Sun and Moon, and that you shall obtain...the perfect projection. Quantum suficit, et quantum appetite*[1]." [2]

> "*The candidate...shall drink [the red liqueur placed upon the Master's altar, thereby] raising his spirit in order to understand the following speech which the Worshipful Master shall address to him at the same time.*

> '*My child, you are receiving the primal matter... Learn that the Great God created before man this primal matter and that*

---
1 "Take as much as you need and as much as you have appetite for."
2 Faulks, Philippa. *The Masonic Magician: The Life and Death of Count Cagliostro and His Egyptian Rite*, P. 214.

he then created man to possess it and be immortal. Man abused

it and lost it, but it still exists in the hands of the Elect of God and from a single grain of this precious matter becomes a projection into infinity.

The acacia which has been given to you at the degree of Master of ordinary Masonry is nothing but that precious matter. And [Hiram's] assassination is the loss of the liquid which you have just received..." [3]

Here, Cagliostro has identified the acacia with the Tree of Eden, which Adam and Eve are said to have abused and subsequently lost after the fall. Again, as with Melissino's rite, we see the treatment of DMT as both the perfect ashlar of Masonry and the philosopher's stone of Alchemy. However, by treating Hiram Abiff as being consubstantial with the sprig of acacia, Cagliostro has carried this symbolism one step further.

It is notable that both Melissino and Cagliostro were initiates of the Rite of Strict Observance, which contains its own potential allusions to the psychoactive properties of acacia. See, for example, the following excerpt from the *Oration from the Reception of a Master Mason*:

"As those who sought the [philosopher's?] stone wanted to climb, in order to retrieve it, one grasped a hold of the green sprig or [Acacia][4] *branch, which pulled out of the ground, when they observed that it had no roots. This made them think that this branch must signify something..."* [5]

Note that DMT is found primarily in the roots of the acacia. This branch must have signified something indeed.

Our detractors have argued that Cagliostro's libation of acacia is purely symbolic. But why, we ask, would a purely symbolic act be described in the precise terms which one would expect had the same act been carried out literally? Cagliostro writes that his candidates for initiation "shall drink" a liqueur prepared from acacia, the "primal matter," thereby 'raising his spirit in order to understand.' This is exactly the type of language which one would expect if Cagliostro was actually, not symbolically, initiating his candidates with an entheo-

---

3   *Ibid.* at 225.
4   The original text gives *Cassia*.
5   De Hoyos, Arturo. *The Rite of Strict Observance and Two High Degree Rituals of the Eighteenth Century*, P. 37

genic libation of acacia. The compound definitely satisfies the requirements of 'raising one's spirit' and imparting a certain 'understanding' that comes only from the type of inebriation induced by ingesting the drug. If not for its DMT content, we cannot conceive of any practical reason why the count would have his acolytes literally drink an ayahuasca-like concoction of acacia. Moreover, Cagliostro's ritual later adds that wine may be substituted for the red liqueur – a clear indication that the intended red elixir was something other than common wine. This was clearly no symbolic act.

Granted there is no mention made in Cagliostro's Egyptian Rite of a MAOI-containing plant, which would normally be necessitated in order to render DMT orally active, as in the case of the Amazonian jungle brew ayahuasca. However, there are yet other possibilities. The first is that, if enough is consumed, the DMT may be able to overwhelm the monoamine oxidase within the gut, thereby making it orally active without the addition of an MAOI. The second possibility is that, being Beta-carbolines, certain flavonoids present in some species of acacia (such as *Acacia confusa*) may work as functioning MAOIs. More investigation is required, and one modern day practicing Alchemist, J. Erik LaPort, author of *Cracking the Philosopher's Stone and Keys to the Kingdom of Alchemy*, is currently doing some important research in this arena.

There is still yet a third possibility, one that is considerably more complicated – as well as bizarre. The following solution has been found in a fascinating and indeed the most curious of places: on the luminous surface of a crystal ball. We must credit our Brother and colleague Michael S. Downs of Georgia for aiding us in piecing the following together.

Amidst the second half of the nineteenth century, during a time that has come to be known as the *occult revival*, the curious practice of spirit communication was spreading like ectoplasm. From séances and psychic channelings to magic mirrors and table tippings, Spiritualism and communications with the dead became all the rage on both sides of the pond, greatly influencing the thought and occupying the minds of those who would contribute largely to the esoteric literature of the era. One of the primary modes of spirit communication that was widely practiced at the time was crystal or mirror gazing, known as *catoptromancy* or *skrying*. This was accomplished with the use of prayers, invocations, and the burning of psychotropic incenses, as well as the consumption of a number of narcotic, hypnagogic, and entheogenic plants and substances. These include but are not limited to cannabis, opium, nitrous oxide, and even psychedelic fungi. (Britten, p. 136) It is believed by practitioners of the art that the spirits of all manner of deceased and disincarnate figures may be called into the crystal or mirror, and thereafter petitioned for the knowledge, favors, etc., that the querent requires or desires. Some of the key players during this creative period include visionary Rosicrucian P.B. Randolph, psychic Spiritualist Emma Hardinge Britten,[6] Helena Petrovna Blavatsky of the Theosophical Society, and especially Freemasons Frederick Hockley and his students Kenneth R.H. Mackenzie and F.G. and Herbert Irwin.

Concerning these last, John Yarker, in his paper *The Society of the Rosy Cross*, provides a description of what he considers to be the various stages of true occult progress, the third of which includes "the use of the 'Crystal Stone' or magical mirror."[7] The association of crystal balls, seeing stones, and magical mirrors with Rosicrucianism goes at least as far back as the publication of the first Rosicrucian manifesto *Fama Fraternitatis* in the early 17th century, wherein is described a 'Vault' having seven sides or walls, and each wall being a door that opens to a chest in which contained among other things "looking glasses of diverse virtues."[8] Yarker claims in the same paper that he knew of only three *Fratres* who possessed any competent and practical knowledge of Rosicrucianism: Frederick Hockley, Kenneth R.H. Mackenzie, and Capt. F.G. Irwin, all three of whom are known to have been avid crystal and mirror gazers.

Frederick Hockley was a highly influential British occultist who divided his time between transcribing magical manuscripts and practicing 'crystallomancy,' as he called it, which is described by him as the art of "invoking by magic crystals or mirrors." Hockley was a pupil of Francis Barrett, author of the celebrated grimoire *The Magus*, and himself the author of at least one book on the subject of magic crystal or mirror gazing. Hockley's Rosicrucian ties went unquestioned to such an extent that he was admitted to the Grade of *Adeptus Exemptus* in the SRIA by Capt. Irwin, even without Hockley's ever having attended a single meeting. The extent to which he experimented with entheogens is unclear, but we do know that he had in his possession at the time of his death a recipe for a mirror-gazing incense, borrowed from *The Book of Oberon*, which contained hashish as an ingredient.

Kenneth R.H. Mackenzie was a hedonistic student of Hockley and a correspondent of French occultist Eliphas Levi. Mackenzie believed to such a degree in the truth of 'crystallomancy' that the source which he used for the entry on the mysterious *Fratres Lucis* in his *Royal Masonic Cyclopaedia* was none other than the disembodied spirit of Cagliostro which had been 'called' into the crystal and subsequently interrogated by Capt. F.G. Irwin's son, Herbert![9]

Regarding Mackenzie, in 1873 Hockley wrote the following:

"I have the utmost reluctance even to refer to Mr. Kenneth Mack-

---

6   Emma Hardinge Britten is believed to have been Hockley's seeress, Britten was also present at the Spiritualist meeting which led to the formation of the Theosophical Society.
7   Yarker, John. *The Society of the Rose Cross*.
8   Yates, Frances A. *The Rosicrucian Enlightenment*, P. 307.
9   Deveney, John Patrick. *Paschal Beverly Randolph: A Nineteenth Century Black American Spiritualist, Rosicrucian, and Sex Magician*, P. 135.

enzie. *I made his acquaintance about 15 or 16 years since. I found him then a very young man who having been educated in Germany possessed a thorough knowledge of German and French and his translations having been highly praised by the press, exceedingly desirous of investigating the Occult Sciences, and when sober one of the most companionable persons I ever met.*"[10]

Very little is known about Capt. F.G. Irwin, but what can be gathered from his correspondence with Hockley, Mackenzie, and others is that he was apparently very active in his Mother Lodge as well as the SRIA College to which he belonged. But, following the death of his son Herbert, who died of a laudanum overdose during a 'crystallomancy' session, F.G. Irwin spent much of his time attempting to contact the spirit of his deceased son. Unfortunately, F.G. Irwin's efforts to contact his deceased son were in vain.

Directly involved in the formation of the SRIA, Hockley, Mackenzie, and the Irwins, are known to have preoccupied themselves with all things Rosicrucian, central to which, they believed, based on a passage in the Rosicrucian manifestos regarding "looking glasses of diverse virtues," was the use of the magic mirror and/or crystal ball. Furthermore, of particular interest to them was the elusive *Fratres Lucis*, an alleged splinter group of *Der Ordens des Gold und Rosenkreuzer*, the first Rosicrucian Order to surface following the initial publication of the *Rosicrucian Manifestos*. Keen to acquire information of the mysterious Fratres Lucis, the same of which was wanting for them on the physical plane, the Irwins put to use their master Hockley's teachings and turned to the crystal ball in order to petition the great mystic Count Cagliostro for assistance. For, it was believed by them that Cagliostro was a *bona fide* member of the Fraternity. As F.G. Irwin's magical diaries of the time clearly reflect, the operations were a great success, and the extended results can be found in Herbert Irwin's *Book of Magic*, the purported astral grimoire of the Fratres Lucis.

Among the alleged Cagliostro crystallomancy transmissions, is one of particular interest to us for our present purposes; one which potentially provides a solution to the problem of the oral activity of the concoction of acacia given to candidates by Cagliostro in his Egyptian Rite of Freemasonry. As we explained earlier, acacia would not normally be orally active. In order for it to become so, the acacia would necessitate being paired with an MAOI-containing plant such as *Peganum harmala*, aka *Syrian rue*. Remarkably, "Herb Rue" is precisely what Herbert Irwin has recorded in his *Book of Magic* as being an important tool in the Fratres Lucis' pharmacopeia, according to the Cagliostro crystallomancy transmissions. The Irwins' master Hockley himself was even fascinated by the "Herb Rue," as can be ascertained from the following excerpt

---

10   Howe, Ellic. *Fringe Masonry in England* 1870-85.

from a letter from Hockley to the Irwins wherein the former pressed the latter for information pertaining to the mysterious "Herb Rue."

> *"There is a recipe on the properties of the plant Rue I know you will allow Herbert to copy out for me as I wish…to try it."*[11]

> *"As I mentioned in my note I read your MSS with very great interest. …When you are in town bring the [Book of Magic] MSS up and we will compare notes…by the bye I asked you for a copy of the recipe on the herb Rue. It is only a few lines."*[12]

That fact that Hockley requested a *recipe*, and not a single herb, is very interesting. But, was Syrian rue truly the plant intended by the Cagliostro transmissions? According to the Roman historian Pliny the Elder, the only difference between Syrian rue and traditional rue is that the latter is the cultivated form of the former.[13] Complicating matters considerably, in Pliny's time no real distinction was made between the two beyond the belief that Syrian rue (or *Peganum harmala*) was the wild manifestation of the cultivated traditional rue (or *Ruta graveolens*). Traditional rue would certainly have been well known to Cagliostro and to the Irwins, the same having extensive and well-documented medicinal as well as religious applications. However, provided that the other botanicals itemized by Herbert Irwin in the *astral* Fratres Lucis pharmacopeia are either psychoactive or are commonly used as substitutes for psychoactive plants, e.g. saffron, opium poppy, vervain, etc., all of which have a long history of use as additives to magical incenses, love philtres, flying ointments, etc., traditional rue would appear completely out of place. Syrian rue, on the other hand, would seem to us to be a perfectly natural, comfortable addition, because it is an MAOI containing plant, where as traditional rue is not. Further, the effects of "Herb Rue" provided in Herbert's *Book of Magic* are consistent with those of Syrian rue, which include sweating, mental clarity, and mood enhancement. According to the *Book of Magic*,

> *"[Herb Rue] is most strengthening and health giving, it imparts life and strength to the body – it opens the pores of the skin and inclines the body to sweat – it is well for diseases of the brain for it imparts strength of all desirable parts."*[14]

---

11   Hamill, John. *The Rosicrucian Seer: Magical Writings of Frederick Hockley*, P. 64.
12   *Ibid.* at 66.
13   Taylor, Joan E. *The Essenes, the Scrolls, and the Dead Sea*, P. 316.
14   Irwin, Herbert. *Book of Magic*, P. 93.

The portion regarding "diseases of the brain" is especially interesting as MAOIs are commonly used in psychiatry to treat mental health disorders including clinical depression and bipolar disorder. The same cannot be said of traditional rue, however.

Regardless of one's attitude concerning crystal balls, magic mirrors, and the obtaining of knowledge from deceased or disincarnate sources, the remarkable consistencies surrounding these transmissions and their content cannot be easily disregarded.

DMT AND THE FRATRES LUCIS

The final example of a Masonic rite alluding to acacia-produced DMT, which we'll here discuss comes from the rituals of the *Fratres Lucis* proper. Recall that Cagliostro himself was believed by many to have been a bona-fide member of the Fratres Lucis, so much so that, in writing his *Royal Masonic Cyclopaedia*, Kenneth R.H. Mackenzie, along with F.G. and Herbert Irwin, resorted to nothing short of conjuring the spirit of the then deceased Cagliostro to visible appearance within a crystal ball for the purpose of questioning him on the nature and history of the Fratres Lucis.[1]

Compare the following excerpt from the first degree of the actual Fratres Lucis with those from Cagliostro's Egyptian Rite.

> "Before receiving thee into the Order they took thee into a darkened room, this teaches thee that our Matter is found in a black state -- our Earth. We also took away all the Metals thou hadst upon thee; this shows that our Matter is not found where Metals grow. They tookest away thy clothing; it shows that our Matter is stripped of the Veil with which Nature has clothed it ...Thine eyes were blindfolded; which teaches that though our Matter is luminous and in itself shining and clear, yet that it is only to be found in the darkest dwelling. A [Cable Tow] was round thy neck, by which the body was led; it...teaches the drawing out of our Matter. ...The point of a [Poniard] was applied to thy breast to warn thee to beware of it. It should remind thee that no double edged weapon [need] be used to slay our Hiram and produce his precious blood, which is shown afterwards by a feeble Brother and his bloody handkerchief... In touching thee with the Compasses (held over a plate with blood thereon), the plate of blood held up, signifies that we have another [Poniard] beside the one that was shown to thee, and which we thrust into the bosom of our Matter until it pours forth blood. ...Hiram, which signifies our Matter, has been killed by Three Workmen, in order that they might procure the Word...

---

1 Deveney, P. 135

> *These traitors buried him and have already his Caput Mortuum. They make a hillock and the dead head appears, as if the Spirits excited it with rage, this is shown by the Branch of Acacia."* [2]

The Fratres Lucis lecture relates an Alchemical application of Masonic ritual which again clearly points to the production of DMT from acacia. Here, as in Cagliostro's ritual, Hiram is treated consubstantially with the acacia. In both, the DMT-rich solution which is extracted from the acacia, our primal matter, prior to the solution's evaporation to a crystalline salt, is identified as 'Hiram's blood,' called by Cagliostro the "mercurial part." According to the lecture, the "Matter" is to be found in the earth; that is, with the roots. For, as Ruck pointed out, the highest concentrations of DMT in the acacia are to be found within the root bark. The removal of the clothing or "stripping of the veil with which nature has clothed" the "Matter" is therefore likely the stripping of the superfluous material -- all but the DMT. The 'other poniard' which is "thrust into the bosom of [the] Matter until it pours forth blood" is perhaps an allusion to the (al)chemical solvent used to extract the compound. And, the three workmen may very well allude to the three step extraction process by which DMT is organically manufactured, etc. etc.

The consistencies are undeniable. Perhaps the Irwins were on to something and the Count truly was a bona fide member of the actual – and not *astral* – Fratres Lucis.

---

2   Grand College of Rites. *Fratres Lucis*, P. 52

ENDOGENOUS DMT PRODUCTION AND THE PINEAL GLAND

Remarkably, DMT is not limited to the plant kingdom alone. In his 1997 book *TIHKAL: Tryptamines I Have Known and Loved*, "psychedelic alchemist" Alexander Shulgin declared that

> "DMT is…in this flower here, in that tree over there, and in yon animal. [It] is, most simply, almost everywhere you choose to look."[1]

And yes, if the reader is wondering, DMT also happens to be inside of every human being. For, DMT is actually manufactured by the human organism, and high amounts of the same have been found in the urine and bloodstream of meditating monks, praying nuns, and even schizophrenics.[2] Endogenous DMT production is therefore believed by many scientists to be the physiological basis for mystical experiences, near-death and out of body experiences, and a whole host of subjective phenomena that cannot otherwise be explained or even begin to be explored by modern science.

In an attempt to discover the source and function of endogenous DMT production within the human organism, Rick Strassman, M.D., Clinical Associate Professor of Psychiatry at the University of New Mexico School of Medicine, became the first scientist to conduct governmentally sanctioned research on humans with a scheduled psychedelic since the 1970's. DMT was largely unknown to the modern Western world, up until the publication of Strassman's book *DMT: The Spirit Molecule*. Between 1990 and 1995, Strassman administered some 400 doses of DMT to nearly five dozen human volunteers, and the book documents the project and the doctor's discoveries. The research which led to the publication of Strassman's book was funded by none other than the Scottish Rite Schizophrenia Research Foundation, a subsidiary of the Northern Masonic Jurisdiction. As the story goes, LSD researcher Daniel

---

1   Strassman, Rick. *DMT: The Spirit Molecule: A Doctor's Revolutionary Research into the Biology of Near-Death and Mystical Experiences*. P 42.
2   Horgan, John. *Rational Mysticism*.

ENDOGENOUS DMT PRODUCTION AND THE PINEAL GLAND

Xander Freedman, who passed away in 1993, was a big supporter of Strassman's work and served on the scientific advisory panel of the Scottish Rite Schizophrenia Research Foundation. Freedman advised Strassman to apply for a grant from the foundation and assured him that he would do all he could to get the DMT project funded. For the contemplative Mason, Strassman's book is enthusiastically recommended for further reading.

Among Strassman's discoveries was that the most probable source of endogenous DMT production within humans is most probably the pineal gland. According to Dr. Rick Strassman, the pineal gland

> *"possesses a lens, cornea, and retina. It is light-sensitive and helps regulate body temperature and skin coloration – two basic survival functions intimately related to environmental light."* [3]

This has led to its (the pineal gland) appropriately being called the *third eye*. When the pineal gland senses daylight, it is thought to labor for the production of serotonin, which regulates appetite, mood, body movement, and a number of other regulatory functions. When the pineal does not sense daylight, conversely, it produces instead melatonin, which regulates sleep patterns as well as body coloration. The conditions under which the pineal is suspected to secrete DMT, on the other hand, is considerably more complex.

> *"The most general hypothesis is that the pineal gland produces psychedelic amounts of DMT at extraordinary times in our lives. Pineal DMT production is the physical representation of non-material, or energetic, processes. It provides us with the vehicle to consciously experience the movement of our life-force [read soul] in its most extreme manifestations. Specific examples of this phenomenon are the following:*
>
> *When our individual life force enters our fetal body, the moment in which we become truly human, it passes through the pineal and triggers the first primordial flood of DMT. Later, at birth, the pineal releases more DMT. In some of us, pineal DMT mediates the pivotal experiences of deep meditation, psychosis, and near-death experiences. As we die, the life-force leaves the body through the pineal gland, releasing another flood of this psychedelic spirit molecule."* [4]

---

3   *Ibid.* 60.
4   *Ibid.* 68.

In other words, according to Dr. Strassman's hypothesis, the pineal gland may very well be the *seat of the soul*, and DMT, the catalyst which facilitates the soul's entry into and exit out of the body during birth, death, trauma, and mystical or visionary experiences – a wild speculation that might be easily dismissed, without the testimonies of the indigenous peoples who employ the compound sacramentally, as well as those of Dr. Strassman's research volunteers, who themselves also experienced the *spirit molecule* firsthand. Moreover, on May 23, 2013 Cottonwood Research Foundation Inc. announced that DMT had officially been discovered in the pineal glands of live rats, making Strassman's hypothesis all the more plausible.[5]

Strassman's views are not too dissimilar from those of philosopher and mathematician René Descartes, who postulated a similar function for our mysterious pineal. In his essay *The Inter-Relation of Soul and Body*, Descartes wrote that

> "[a]lthough the soul is joined with the entire body, there is one part of the body [the pineal] in which it exercises its function more than elsewhere. ...[The pineal] is so suspended between the passages containing the animal spirits [guiding reason and carrying sensation and movement] that it can be moved by them...; and it carries this motion on to the soul... Then conversely, the bodily machine is so constituted that whenever the gland is moved in one way or another by the soul, or for that matter by any other cause, it pushes the animal spirits which surround it to the pores of the brain."[6]

Descartes noticed too that the pineal gland happens to be the sole singleton organ within the human brain. Recognizing via personal introspection that thoughts arise only one at a time, Descartes also postulated that the pineal gland is the source of the many thoughts that are aroused within the mind throughout one's life.

It is worth noting that this line of research has shed light not only on the significance of the sprig of acacia within Freemasonry, but also potentially on the Master's *fatal blow*, the same of which strikes in the same general region, albeit superficially, wherein the so-called *seat of the soul*; that is, the pineal gland, resides. It was perhaps with a remarkable flash of insight into this same profound and esoteric knowledge that British Freemason W.L. Wilmshurst so cryptically but eloquently declared in his 1922 classic *The Meaning of Masonry* that

---

5   Cottonwood Research Foundation, Inc. *NEW: DMT Found in the Pineal Gland of Live Rats.*
6   Strassman, P. 60

> "[t]he 'head' of the material organism of man is the spirit of man, and this spirit consciously conjoined with the Universal Spirit is Deity's supreme instrument and vehicle in the temporal world. Such a man's physical organism and brain have become sublimated and keyed up to a condition and an efficiency immensely in advance of average humanity. Physiological processes are involved which cannot be discussed here, beyond saying that in such a man the entire nervous system contributes to charge certain ganglia and light up certain brain-centers in a way of which the ordinary mind knows nothing. ...But the Master Mason, in virtue of his mastership, knows how to control and apply those energies. They culminate and come to self-consciousness in his head, in his intelligence. ...The same truth is...testified to, though...under veils of symbolic phrasing, in the reference to the sprig of acacia planted at the head of the grave of the Masonic Grand Master and prototype, Hiram Abiff. The grave is the candidate's soul; the sprig of acacia typifies the latent akasha (to use an Eastern term) or divine germ planted in that soil and waiting to become quickened into activity in his intelligence, the 'head' of that plane. When that sprig of acacia blooms at the head of his soul's sepulcher, he will understand...the mystery of the death of Hiram. ...It is a mystery of spiritual consciousness, the efflorescence of the mind in God, the opening up of the human intelligence in conscious association with the Universal and Omniscient Mind."[7]

To quote once more from McKenna, who too intuited the significance of DMT in Alchemy and certain "secret societies,"

> "So, how can it be then, that a compound which each of us carries right here, right in the pineal gland, right in the ajna chakra, the philosopher's stone is no further away than that. How can this be secret from us? ...[There] are lots of mystery cults and secret societies in the world, I don't know if any of them are guarding DMT as a secret, it may be so."[8]

In our educated estimation, it is so.

---

7   Wilmshurst, W.L. *The Meaning of Masonry*, P. 150.
8   McKenna, Terence. *Psychedelia: Rap Dancing Into the 3rd Millenium Talk*, 1994

DMT CONCLUSION

The idea that a psychedelic drug could have played a part in early Masonic ritual is often met by members of the Fraternity with repugnance and disbelief. After all, we as Free and Accepted Masons are charged with the task of peacefully submitting to the laws of the land wherein we reside; and, outside of affiliation with the *Santo Daime*, the *Uniao do Vegetal*, or the Native American Church, the only three organizations legally sanctioned to use the compound in our country, DMT production, possession, and consumption are completely illegal in the United States. One must keep in mind, however, that the time in question was the 18th century, when scientific investigation was still in its infancy, long before the "war on drugs" or the notion of psychedelics were even concepts. The detrimental effects of addiction were for the most part still to be seen, as were the hard drugs which are so plaguing society today, such as crack cocaine, heroin, and methamphetamine. Therefore, the stigma which surrounds the use of essentially any drug in this day and age, was for them completely foreign. Thus, the discovery of DMT and its magical effects would have been met with such novelty and excitement that it is no wonder entire Masonic lectures were dedicated to its mysteries.

In our estimation, it is beyond question that a number of Masonic rites allude to the use of DMT produced from acacia in their lectures. What is questionable is how this curiosity of the Craft came to be. Was the sprig of acacia added to Masonic ritual on account of its DMT content, or did certain Alchemically-inclined Freemasons who were privy to the tree's entheogenic mysteries take it upon themselves to interpret and apply it in that manner? We may never know, just as we may never know who, if anyone, was responsible for the cassia/acacia switch in the first place. What we do know, however, is that DMT was not properly synthesized until the 1950s. The possibility that the compound was being extracted and employed by select Freemasons as early as the 18th century is therefore highly significant. Masons have repeatedly touted the Order as a friend and protector of science. Therefore, perhaps for the first time, it is beginning to look as though the Fraternity may have actually made a lasting contribution to the field.

We now conclude this study into the entheogenic potential of the acacia symbol in Masonry with a quote by H.L. Haywood, extracted from vol. III of Albert Mackey's *Encyclopedia of Freemasonry and Its Kindred Sciences*, which quaintly confirms our current conclusion.

> *"It is admitted that the texts and nomenclature of Medieval materials on [Hermetism] were cryptic and queer; but for that there are several explanations for the need for secrecy, [including] the need to keep laymen from endangering themselves with drugs they could not understand."* [1]

Surely, DMT would fall into that category.

---

1   Mackey, Albert G., "Alchimy, The Ordinall of" *Encyclopedia of Freemasonry and Its Kindred Sciences*.

UNION OF THE PLANTS

In addition to the indigenous tribes of the Amazon, ayahuasca is also used within a number of religious organizations stemming from a church known as the *Santo Daime*. The Santo Daime is a syncretic religion that was founded in the 1930s by illiterate rubber-tapper Raimundo Irineu, known within the religion as Meistre Irineu. But, of particular interest to us is the Santo Daime splinter group *União do Vegetal*, meaning *Union of the Plants*, which was founded by another rubber-tapper – and operative mason – Jose Gabriel de Costa some three decades later.

The União do Vegetal (UDV) is a syncretic religion that blends its own form of Amazonian shamanism with Catholicism, Kardecian Spiritism, Freemasonry, Greek mythology, Kabbalah, and Umbanda. Like the Santo Daime before them, the UDV incorporates many symbols that would no doubt be familiar to the Freemason. These include the sun, the moon, and the star. The beehive is also an important symbol. The UDV took the loose Masonic associations of the Santo Daime some steps further not only by applying the concept of degrees to the society, but Meistre Gabriel actually taught that *"Hoasca"* was the gift of Yahweh to King Solomon. How convenient then that we as Masons have indications within our very rituals that point to the ceremonial use of dimethyltryptamine.

One splinter group led by Meistre Joaquim Jose de Andrade Neto, *Centro Espirito Beneficente Ordem Masonica Rosaluz*, has so stressed their Masonic leanings that the church even went so far as to include the qualifier 'Masonic' in their title. However, it must be noted that this group currently considered irregular among Free and Accepted Masons and have no legitimate Masonic ties. They are, however, a tax exempt religious organization in North America.

For some forty years the Santo Daime, UDV, and splinter groups were limited to South America alone, since DMT is listed as a scheduled narcotic in the US and elsewhere. But, following a long battle with the courts, on February 21st, 2006 the Supreme Court of the United States rightfully issued a unanimous decision affirming Religious Liberty in the case of *Gonzales vs. O Centro Espirita Beneficente União do Vegetal*, permitting affiliates of both the

Santo Daime and the União do Vegetal to use ayahuasca in a religious, ceremonial context.

Interlude

Having satisfied myself that DMT was indeed used in various early Masonic rites, and thus may explain the widespread switch from cassia to acacia in the Master Mason ritual in the early to mid-seventeenth century, I decided to turn my attention to other possible examples of entheogenic symbolism that may be concealed within Masonic ritual. I would not be disappointed.

Unbeknownst to most at the time, the substances with which the Alchemists were working with, like Cagliostro and Melissino after them, were psychoactive ones. The stones of the philosophers were none other than vegetable stones; that is, they were crystalline drugs prepared from entheogenic plants such as acacia. The same is true of the Ancient Mysteries, e.g. those of Eleusis and Mithras, etc., many of which are believed by scholars to have employed their own entheogenic sacraments. Because Ancient Craft and certain of the high degrees of Freemasonry clearly borrowed symbols from alchemy and the Mystery Schools, symbolism that explicitly points to psychedelic plants inescapably appears as well in those same degrees.

PART II: ERGOT

MASONRY &
THE MYSTERIES OF ELEUSIS

> *"For it appears to me that among the many exceptional and divine things your Athens has produced and contributed to human life, nothing is better than [the Eleusinian] mysteries. For by means of them we have been transformed from a rough and savage way of life to the state of humanity, and have been civilized. Just as they are called initiations, so in actual fact we have learned from them the fundamentals of life, and have grasped the basis not only for living with joy but also dying with a better hope."*
>
> Marcus, in Cicero, De legibus, 2.14.36[1]

According to the theories of J.S.M. Ward[2], Freemasonry is a continuation of the various Mystery cults which flourished in ancient Egypt, Greece, Rome, Persia – and even India– before they were indiscriminately suppressed in favor of the new, growing, Christian religion, which brought with it its own indomitable version of the 'Sacred Mysteries.' Albert Pike even declared in his *Morals and Dogma* that "Masonry is identical with the ancient Mysteries," though he later added that this is so only to a limited extent. For in Pike's estimation, Masonry is

> *"but an imperfect image of [the Mysteries'] brilliancy, the ruins only of their grandeur, and a system that has experienced progressive alterations, the fruits of social events, political circumstances, and the ambitious imbecility of its improvers."*[3]

It is generally accepted that central to many of these Mysteries, whether they were solar or agrarian in nature, was the indoctrination of their participants regarding the reality of deity and the immortality

---

1   Meyer, Marvin W. *The Ancient Mysteries: A Sourcebook of Sacred Texts.*, P. viii
2   John Sebastian Marlow Ward (1885 – 1949) was an English author who published widely on the subject of Freemasonry and esotericism.
3   De Hoyos, Arturo. *Albert Pike's Morals and Dogma: Annotated Edition.*, P. 96

of the soul.[4] In most cases, these doctrines appear to have been imparted via complex ritualized dramatizations of the traditional myths and legends surrounding the central deity of the cult. During these rituals the candidate himself was oftentimes made consubstantial with the deity, suffering his trials, death, and resurrection – and in some instances, even acting out the deity's undertakings while sojourning through the Land of the Dead. Often, it was precisely these ritualized reenactments that constituted the various ceremonies of Initiation into the ancient Mysteries, the completion of which veritably made one a *bona fide* member of the Mystery cult. Additionally, obligations of secrecy concerning all that had transpired during the ceremony of Initiation were enforced upon everyone present, the breaking of which, participants were duly informed, was punishable by penalty of death.

The most popular of the ancient Mystery cults was indisputably that of the goddess Demeter and her daughter Kore (aka Persephone) which were celebrated at Eleusis, Greece from around 1450 BCE to 392 CE. The myth of this cult narrates the story of the grain goddess Demeter and the lengths to which she was willing to go in order to be reunited with her beloved daughter Persephone. In the myth, Persephone was abducted by the subterranean god Hades (or Pluto) while she was gathering flowers with the other 'Flower Maidens.' In the end, after many tribulations a compromise was reached where Persephone would be permitted to return to the land of the living and reunite with her mother, but only under the condition that she re-descend to the Underworld for one season out of every year – namely, winter – in order reassume her role as the queen of Hades. It was within this narrative of a periodical descent into the Underworld and subsequent return to the realm of the living that the Hierophants at Eleusis communicated to the candidates their cherished doctrine of the immortality of the soul.

The primary celebrations observed at Eleusis are known to have consisted of two separate Mysteries: a *Lesser* and a *Greater*. The Lesser Mystery appears to have been celebrated between the winter solstice and the vernal equinox, and entailed the preliminary indoctrination of the candidates regarding the central myth of the cult. Participation therein constituted the new member a *Mystis* or *Initiate*, and was the mandatory prerequisite which prepared him for admittance into the Greater Mystery. The latter was celebrated between the autumnal equinox and the winter solstice. Unlike the Lesser, it is believed that the Greater Mystery did not involve a lengthy recapitulation of the cult's sacred myth, but rather consisted of something which was *seen* directly – hence the

---

4   Mackey, Albert G. *The Symbolism of Freemasonry*, P. 347.

title of *Epopt* or *Seer* applied to Initiates of this level. Therefore, we can be confident that what the *Mystae only heard* second-hand in the Lesser Mystery, the *Epopt* witnessed or experienced first-hand in the Greater.

Participants in the Greater Mystery were expected to observe certain specific dietary restrictions, such as complete abstinence from foods including fish, legumes, apples, and most especially, pomegranates and "barndoor fowl" – all of which held a special, symbolic significance in regards to the Mysteries of Eleusis. "The pomegranate," for example, says Greek scholar Jane Ellen Harrison, "was dead men's food, and once tasted drew Persephone back to the shades." Similarly, the rooster was said to have been consecrated to the goddess Demeter:

> "Porphyry in his treatise on Abstinence from Animal Food, notes the reason and the rigour of the Eleusinian taboos. Demeter, he says, is a goddess of the lower world and they consecrate the cock to her...We are apt to associate the cock with daylight and his early morning crowing, but the Greeks for some reason regarded the bird as chthonic." [5]

It is due perhaps to these *chthonic* associations that the rooster also happens to be an important symbol within the gloomy *Chamber of Reflection*, where the candidate for Masonic Initiation is caused to tarry for a while prior to taking the first degree. Like Persephone in the Underworld, the candidate being held in the dim Chamber of Reflection is oftentimes surrounded with grim reminders of his own mortality, but as was also the case with Persephone, it is the rooster which heralds the illumination awaiting the candidate upon his release from the Chamber. It is noteworthy that the rooster was also said to have been a favorite pet of the psychopomp Mercury, whose image, according to John Yarker's *The Arcane Schools*, was displayed within the temple at Eleusis along with those of Sol and Luna.[6]

Another important celebration observed at Eleusis was the annual *Haloa* festival which was celebrated in honor of both Demeter and Dionysus in and around the winter solstice. This celebration, which Harrison called "the very counterpart" to the Eleusinian Mysteries, took place on Triptolemus'[7] threshing-floor, where the sacred barley grown on the Rarian plain, the same of which would be used to make the

5   Sorabji, Richard. *Animal Minds and Human Morals: The Origins of the Western Debate.* P. 82.
6   Yarker, John. *The Arcane Schools*, P. 100
7   Triptolemus was a demi-god of the Eleusinian mysteries who presided over the sowing of grain and the milling of wheat.

mysterious *kykeon* potion drunk during the Greater Mystery, was ceremonially threshed. According to Harrison,

> *"The affiliation of the worship of the corn-goddess to that of the wine-god is of the first importance. The coming of Dionysos brought a new spiritual impulse to the religion of Greece...and it was to this new impulse that the Eleusinian Mysteries owed... their ultimate dominance. Of [the Eleusinian Mysteries] the Haloa is, I think, the primitive prototype. As to the primitive gist of the Haloa, there is no shadow of a doubt: the name speaks for itself. Harpocration rightly explains the festival, 'the Haloa gets is name, according to Philochorus, from the fact that people hold sports at the threshing-floors, and he says it is celebrated in the month of Poseidon.'... [That] the Haloa was celebrated in the month of Poseidon [is] a fact as surprising as it is ultimately significant. What has a threshing festival to do with mid-winter, when all the grain should be safely housed in the barns? Normally, as in ancient days, the threshing follows as soon as may be after the cutting of the corn; it is threshed and afterwards winnowed in the open threshing-floor, and in mid-winter is no time even in Greece for an open-air operation. The answer is simple. The shift of date is due to Dionysos. The rival festivals of Dionysos were in mid-winter. He possessed himself of the festivals of Demeter, took over her threshing-floor and compelled the anomaly of a winter threshing festival. The latest time that a real threshing festival could take place is Pyanepsion, but by Poseidon it is just possible to have an early Pithoigia and to revel with Dionysos. There could be no clearer witness to the might of the incoming god."* [8]

It may be surprising to some to learn that the threshing-floor also happens to be an important symbol within Freemasonry. In the lectures of the so-called 'American Ritual,' which Mackey lamented as "being lost or becoming obsolete" even in his day, the candidate for Masonic Initiation is described as one who is travelling "to the threshing-floor of Ornan the Jebusite, where language was restored and Masonry found". The association of Ornan's threshing-floor with Freemasonry stems from the fact that King Solomon's temple was said to have been erected on that very same site. According to the story in 1 Chronicles, the land had

---

[8] Harrison, Jane Ellen. *Prolegomena to the Study of Greek Religion*, P. 146-147.

earlier been purchased from Ornan by King David, Solomon's father, for the purpose of erecting there an altar, whereon David was to make sacrificial offerings after witnessing a vision of the "angel of the Lord" whom was seen standing within the vicinity of the threshing-floor. Before that time, all sacrifices would have generally been made on the 'altar of the burnt offering' which was housed in the tabernacle. However, following David's sacrifice, it was decreed that a permanent temple should be erected atop Ornan's threshing-floor – a temple which would eventually come to replace the 'tabernacle in the wilderness' as the domicile of the Jewish deity. It is this permanent temple wherein the various degrees of Ancient Craft Masonry symbolically take place. Therefore, it was said of the candidate for Masonic Initiation that he is allegorically travelling "to the threshing-floor of Ornan," that is, the temple of Solomon the King. The threshing-floor is thus implicative of Initiation and the Masonic Lodge. Other important symbols connecting Masonry to the Mysteries celebrated at Eleusis can be found in the lectures of the Fellowcraft degree.

Further, on his symbolic *passage* to the *middle chamber* of the temple, the attention of the newly-made Fellowcraft is directed toward a curious image: *a sheaf of wheat suspended near the bank of a river*. The word associated with it, which can be translated either as *an ear of corn* or *a stream of water*, is equally curious. As Pike pointed out in his *The Book of Words*,

> "We do not know when this word was adopted, and no one has ever been able to find any especial significance in it as a Masonic word. But I am entirely satisfied that there was originally a concealed significance in every word used in a Masonic degree. Some secret meaning and application was covered and concealed by each of them." [9]

The explanation provided for the word in question is similarly obscure. According to Mackey, "the Gileadites under Jephthah made use of [this word] as a test at the passage of the river Jordan after a victory over the Ephramites," but Pike was admittedly not so convinced: "We fail now to see the application to anything in Free-Masonry of the account given by the Hebrew chronicler of the use made of this word, by which to detect the men of a particular Tribe, who pronounced it differently from others." Robert Hewitt Brown was likewise suspicious of the traditional explanation provided for the word in question, and in his 1882 book *Stellar Theology and Masonic Astrology* he offered an alternative interpretation:

---

9   Pike, Albert. *The Book of the Words*, P. 47-48

"A reference to the Eleusinian Mysteries will go far to clear up [the probable true meaning of 'ears of corn hanging by a water-ford,' or 'a sheaf of wheat suspended near the bank of a river,'] and give us the true import of this symbol. The Eleusinian Mysteries were derived from those of Isis, who was known to the Greeks by the name of Ceres, and also Cybele. Ceres, or Cybele, was the goddess of the harvest, and was represented, like the beautiful virgin of the zodiac, bearing spears of ripe corn. In like manner, Isis was with the Egyptians emblematic of the harvest season. In the Egyptian zodiac Isis occupied the place of Virgo, and was represented with three ears of corn in her hand. The Syrian word for an ear of corn is 'sibola'... This word also means 'a stream of water,' and the emblem of ears of corn or a sheaf of wheat near a water-course, or river, was one of the emblems of the Eleusinian and Tyrian (or Dionysiac) Mysteries. As the word had a double meaning, the picture formed a rebus. The river is the river Nile, the overflow of which enriched the soil and brought forth the abundant harvests of Egyptian corn, all of which was symbolically represented by the ears of corn hanging by a river." [10]

Another noteworthy symbol found in the Fellowcraft degree which is readily relatable to the Mysteries celebrated at Eleusis include "those two famous, brazen pillars" between which the candidate at one point in the ritual is caused to pass.

King Solomon's temple was said to have been fitted with two impressive, brazen pillars – one called *Boaz* and the other, *Jachin* – which were set in temple's outer portico as symbols of *strength* and *establishment*. In addition to the terrestrial and celestial globes which were placed upon their summit, we are told that those two magnificent pillars were lavishly ornamented with "a representation of net-work, lily-work, and pomegranates." In the Fellowcraft degree the candidate is informed that these decorations "are said to denote Unity, Peace, and Plenty," for "[t]he net-work, from its connection, denotes unity; the lily-work, from its whiteness, and the retired place in which it grows, purity and peace; the pomegranates, from the exuberance of their seed, denote plenty." However, all three of them also happen to be symbols associated with the Mysteries celebrated at Eleusis. In the Homeric *Hymn to Demeter*, the lily was specifically named as being among the flowers gathered by Persephone at the moment of her fateful abduction. Similarly, it was her naïve acceptance of

---

10   Brown, Robert Hewitt. Stellar Theology and Masonic Astrology, P. 155.

the seeds of the pomegranate which secured for Hades Persephone's annual return to the Land of the Dead. The accompanying net-work, too, can be related directly back to the story of Persephone's abduction. In Greek mythology, nets are associated with the goddess Britomartis, the daughter of Eubulus and thus the grand-daughter of Demeter – both of whom were prominent figures within the Eleusinian Mysteries. In the third installment of Callimachus' *Hymn to Artemis*, we read of Britomartis' desperate retreat into the nets of some nearby fishermen in a final attempt to evade the ruthless advances of her pursuer King Minos of Crete. Following this episode, the goddess Britomartis came to be known fittingly as *Diktyanna* or *the Lady of the Nets*. According to chronoligist Edward Greswell,

> *"[T]he Britomartis of Crete...was absolutely the antitype of the Kore of Eleusis; and...she was originally conceived and proposed in the same relation to the Cretan Deo, as the Kore to the Eleusinian Demeter...We see too that as the Kore in her proper fable was represented as in danger from the violence of Aïdoneus or Pluto, so was this Britomartis in the Cretan one, as similarly in danger from the violence of Minos; and as the Kore succumbs to this violence in her proper fable, and is actually carried away, so does this Britomartis in the Cretan fall a victim to that of Minos, though not in the same way, by being carried underground, but by being forced into the sea [in fishing nets]. The same physical truth both might be, and probably was, adumbrated by each of these representations, only from a different point of view. The authors of the Grecian fable looked on the principle of vegetable life as residing chiefly in the ground; the authors of the Cretan looked a little deeper, and discovered, as they thought, the true principle and first beginnings of vegetable life, in the moisture of the ground imbibed by the seed; in the aqueous principle, the true pabulum of vegetable life in every form and shape; in the rains and the dews, from which the earth derived its moisture, and in the sea, as the ultimate source and fountain-head of both. And therefore with a stricter regard to the absolute order, connection, and dependencies of things, they chose to represent their Britomartis as lost at first in the sea, and as recovered at last from the sea."* [11]

---

11 Greswell, Edward. *Origines Kalendariae Hellenicae*, P. 376.

The symbolic representations of the net-work, lily-work, and pomegranates which adorned the pillars that were said to have been set within the outer portico of King Solomon's temple allude therefore not only to the concepts of "Unity, Peace, and Plenty" referenced in the Fellowcraft degree, but are also indicative of the Mysteries celebrated at Eleusis, wherein one was chiefly indoctrinated regarding the immortality of the soul.

The reality of deity and the immortality of the soul were in all probability the primary doctrines intended to be imparted during most, if not all of the Mysteries, including those celebrated at Egypt, Greece, Rome, Persia, India, and elsewhere about the globe. In the case of those celebrated at Eleusis, the participants were instructed via a ritualized dramatization of the central myth associated with the goddess Demeter and her daughter Persephone, wherein the candidate was made consubstantial with the latter in his symbolic descent into the Land of the Dead and miraculous return to the realm of the living. In the author's estimation, it is no mere coincidence that Masonry requires of Her Initiates a belief in this same ideology. The adopted means of imparting those concepts, too, have their origin nowhere but in the rites and ceremonies observed during the celebration of the ancient Mysteries.

THRESHING FLOORS AND WATERFALLS

In the previous chapter, we explained that Freemasonry has been described as a continuation of the various Mystery cults which flourished in ancient Rome, Egypt, Persia, and especially Greece before they were indiscriminately suppressed in favor of the new, growing, Christian religion. As Albert Mackey explained, central to these Mysteries, whether they were solar or agrarian in nature, was the indoctrination of their participants regarding the reality of deity and the immortality of the soul.

It was stated in the previous chapter that what the *Mystis* learned via an allegorical representation was only secondhand knowledge, but the knowledge that the *Epopt possessed was gained through direct experience.* Where the *Mystis* once had faith, the *Epopt* possessed *gnosis*. Since we can safely assume that the reality of deity and the immortality of the soul were the central lessons allegorically imparted to the initiates of the Lesser Mystery, the question naturally begs to be answered: short of physical death, how does one provide firsthand experience of God and of the afterlife? How does one induce in another the experience of the latter's soul being veritably freed from the bonds of the material plane and allowed to wander in the Underworld or in the Heavens where the Glory of God may be beheld directly? For, this is the type of experience that was reportedly induced in participants of the Greater Mystery. According to Sophocles,

> "[t]hrice happy are those of mortals, who having seen those rites depart for Hades; for to them alone is it granted to have true life there; to the rest all there is evil."[1]

---

1 Eyer, Shawn. *Psychedelic Effects and the Eleusinian Mysteries.*

Similarly, Pindar exclaimed:

> *"Happy is he who, having seen the rites, goes below the hollow earth; for he knows the end of life and he knows its god-sent beginning."* [2]

Plutarch went into considerably more detail.

> *"[Upon dying] the soul suffers an experience similar to those who celebrate the great initiations... Wanderings astray in the beginning, tiresome walking in circles, some frightening paths in darkness that lead nowhere; then immediately before the end all the terrible things, panic and shivering and sweat, and amazement. And then some wonderful light comes to meet you, pure regions and meadows are there to greet you, with sounds and dances and solemn, sacred words and holy views; and there the initiate, perfect by now, set free and loose from all bondage, walks about, crowned with a wreath, celebrating the festival together with the other sacred and pure people, and he looks down on the uninitiated, unpurified crowd in this world in mud and fog beneath his feet."* [3]

Finally, Proclus described his experience in the Greater Mystery as follows:

> *"They cause the sympathy of the souls with the ritual in a way that is incomprehensible to us, and divine, so that some of the initiands are stricken with panic, being filled with divine awe; others assimilate themselves to the holy symbols, leave their own identity, become at home with the gods, and experience divine possession."* [4]

The problem of what could have so consistently induced an experience that convinced thousands upon thousands of participants, including even the most intelligent of philosophers, of the reality of the vision shared by all *Epopts* of the Greater Mystery at Eleusis has plagued scholars and scientists for centuries. It was not until the publication of Wasson, Hofmann, and Ruck's remarkable book *The Road to Eleusis: Unveiling the Secret of the Mysteries* in 1978 that a feasible explanation was finally set forth. In said work, the authors offered the proposal that such an experience could only be induced so consistently and

---

2   Ibid.
3   Ibid.
4   Ibid.

reliably with the use of an entheogenic compound; that is, with a psychedelic drug.

This is actually not very surprising. The notion that an entheogenic compound of some sort had been employed at Eleusis was entertained as early as the 1920s by Freemason and philosopher Edouard Schure, who, in addition to making an attempt to revive the ancient Mysteries, actually postulated for the source of the Eleusinian experience an intoxicating, visionary incense. Religious studies scholar Houston Smith and poet Robert Graves also imagined a psychoactive drug as the source of the visions suffered at Eleusis. The use of entheogenic compounds in ritualistic settings is perhaps one of the most commonly employed initiatory motif in indigenous and semi-civilized societies. In the Amazon Basin it is *ayahuasca*, among the Mazatecs, *teonanacatl*, with the ancient Vedantists, it was *soma*, and with the Parsis, it was *haoma* which accomplishes (or accomplished) this experience. But, in all of these cases and more it was or is an entheogenic compound which facilitates (or facilitated) the experience.

An important distinction needs to be made here. In the science and art of initiation there are actually two different types of initiation: *formal* and *actual*. Formal initiation plants the seeds and provides the means by which, through time and application of the lessons inculcated, those seeds might blossom into actual initiation or illumination. However, not all formal initiates attain actual initiation, nor have all actual initiates been formally initiated. The only way to ensure that both formal initiation and actual initiation coincide in the same moment is to have a failsafe means by which actual initiation may be induced upon being formally initiated. It is this function which psychedelic drugs served in the ancient Mysteries and still serve to this day in certain indigenous and semi-civilized societies.

Select entheogenic compounds have the effect of expanding one's consciousness in such a way that previously abstract and ineffable notions of deity and spirit become at once tangible and concrete to the extent that there can be no question of the reality of the spiritual plane or planes. The experiences reported by those who have experimented with such compounds consistently involve motifs of astral travel, near death experiences, perception of the unity of all creation and the immanence of God, contact with angelic or divine beings, etc. In the metaphysical words of esteemed Freemason Swami Vivekananda,

> "[m]atter is represented by the ether; when the action of Prana is most subtle, this very ether, in the finer state of vibration, will represent the mind, and there it will be still one unbroken mass. If you can simply get into that subtle vibration, you will see and feel that the whole universe is composed of subtle vibrations.*

Sometimes certain drugs have the power to take us, while as yet in the senses, to that condition." [5]

Just as at Eleusis, what one was once required to accept on faith, he has now been given direct knowledge of the reality or unreality of those same particulars.

In the Mysteries celebrated at Eleusis, the compound which accomplished this *actual* initiation in its participants was called *kykeon* and, according to Wasson *et al.*, was prepared from barley which had been infested with *Claviceps purpurea* or ergot. Ergot, a term which stems from the French word *argot* meaning *cock's spur*, is a fungus which infects cereal grasses and grains including but not limited to barley, wheat, and corn. In the Middle Ages it was responsible for the death of countless individuals who had eaten bread or other foods which had been prepared from ergot infested grains. Symptoms of ergot poisoning, otherwise known as *St. Anthony's Fire*, are gruesome in the extreme and include intense and alternating feelings of heat and cold, the development of gangrene resulting in loss of limb, delirious hallucinations, and severe gastric disturbances usually ending in death. However, also present within the ergot kernel are certain other alkaloids which have been known to induce ecstatic euphoria in numberless users. For, it was in an attempt to discover a cure for this dreaded ergot poisoning and other ailments (including migraine and respiratory illness) that led Swiss chemist Albert Hofmann to the discovery of LSD-25 in the 1930s.

As in the Greater Mystery at Eleusis, those under the influence of LSD experience alternating panic, shivering, sweat, amazement, visions of light, awe, ego death, boundary dissolution, heavenly ascent, chthonic descent, contact with angels and divine beings, etc. Remarkably, unlike the toxic compounds which are responsible for the severe and detrimental symptoms associated with ergot poisoning, the psychoactive alkaloids which would later be known as LSD are water soluble, and, according to Merkur, Webster, and others, could have been removed from the poisonous alkaloids present in ergot by using a simple and primitive water extraction.

Shawn Eyer, Past Master of Academia Lodge No. 847 in Oakland, CA, wrote in his paper *Psychedelic Effects and the Eleusinian Mysteries,*

> *"the secret of what really happened at Eleusis remains one of the premier problems for historians of religion. That a trance state played an important role in the initiation is being suggested by more and more scholars. While there are various possible means of entering a mind-altering state of consciousness resembling that*

---
5   Vivekananda, Swami. *Raja Yoga*, P. 35.

described in ancient sources, the use of a botanical stimulus is by far the most reliable. The model expressed by R. Gordon Wasson, Albert Hofmann, and Carl Ruck must therefore be taken seriously. Their theory is the first truly realistic explanation for the most-documented aspect of the sacred mysteries; their profound, beneficial, and lasting effects upon the millions of initiates who, at one time or another, stood enraptured on the steps of the torch-lit Telesterion [at Eleusis]." [6]

The *Hymn to Demeter* gives the constituents of kykeon specifically as barley groats, pennyroyal mint leaves, and water, none of which, besides the negligible thujone count present in the pennyroyal, are known to be notably psychoactive.[7] However, supposing the barley had been infested with *Claviceps purpurea*, a tea made from the same would produce an entheogenic beverage that would have induced heavenly visions in even the most obstinate of participants. It is this same possibility that we intend to explore within the context of Freemasonry.

In his book *Secrets of Eleusis*, Carl A.P. Ruck, the professor of Classics at Boston University, argued that the ergot used to prepare the sacred kykeon potion was harvested from the Rarian plain which grew adjacent to Eleusis and was then ceremonially separated from the barley shafts upon what was known as Triptolemos' Threshing Floor.[8] A threshing floor is a circular space out in the open where grains, after being harvested and dried, are smashed with mallets and thrown into the open wind (a process known as *winnowing*). The grains of wheat, being heavier, fall to the threshing floor to be collected, while the less weighty chaff is blown away by the ensuing wind. On Triptolemos' Threshing Floor, however, it was the kernels of ergot which were collected, and not necessarily the wheat. Significantly, the threshing floor also happens to be an important symbol within Freemasonry.

As previously discussed, the association of Ornan's threshing floor with Freemasonry stems from the fact that King Solomon's temple was said to have been erected on that very same site. The land had earlier been purchased from Ornan by King David, Solomon's father, for the purpose of erecting there an altar, whereon David was to make sacrificial offerings after witnessing a vision of the "angel of the Lord" whom was seen standing within the vicinity of the threshing floor. Before that time, all sacrifices would have generally been made on the 'altar of the burnt offering' which was housed in the tabernacle.

---

6   Eyer, Shawn. *Psychedelic Effects and the Eleusinian Mysteries.*
7   Hopkinson, N. *Callimachus' Hymn to Demeter*, P. 87.
8   Ruck, Carl A.P. *Sacred Mushrooms of the Goddess and the Secrets of Eleusis*, P. 121-45.

However, following David's sacrifice, it was decreed that a permanent temple should be erected atop Ornan's threshing floor; a temple which would eventually come to replace the 'tabernacle in the wilderness' as the domicile of the Jewish deity. It is this permanent temple wherein the various degrees of Ancient Craft Masonry symbolically take place. Therefore, it was said of the candidate for Masonic Initiation that he is allegorically travelling "to the threshing-floor of Ornan," that is, the temple of Solomon the King. The threshing floor is thus implicative of Initiation in a Masonic Lodge and the "ground floor" of King Solomon's temple.

Amazingly, King Solomon's temple can be directly associated with ergot and thus with kykeon. In Dan Merkur's daring book *The Mystery of Manna* he outlines what he calls the *draught ordeal* from the *Old Testament* book of *Numbers*. In this Biblical episode two women are brought into the tabernacle, one of whom is known to be an adulteress, while the other is only suspected of adultery. At her trial, the former woman is given a beverage to drink which, since she is guilty, she is told, will cause her thigh to "drop off" and her stomach to "swell." If the reader will recall, gangrenous loss of limb and severe gastric disturbances were among the symptoms listed which characterize ergot poisoning. Notably, the drink given to the unfortunate woman was prepared in no other way than to collect up dust from the floor which was then added to water, the very dust which in the same episode is then offered by the priests as a "cereal offering" before Yahweh, thereby identifying the floor of the tabernacle as a threshing floor, just like the "ground floor" of King Solomon's temple. This should come as no surprise to Freemasons, since in the Entered Apprentice degree we are informed unequivocally that the tabernacle "was an exact model of Solomon's temple." If the model was truly exact, then naturally it would have been established, just like Solomon's temple, upon a threshing floor. In the words of Dr. Merkur,

> *"On the conventional assumption that the floor of the tabernacle was a projection into the era of Moses of the floor of the Jerusalem temple, the concern with a cereal offering suggests the sort of dust that would have been found on the threshing floor of [Ornan], which the Jerusalem sanctuary had once been. Implicitly, dust such as would have been left on a floor where grain was threshed was added to holy water. ...The toxic dust that was taken from the threshing floors and mixed with water for the cereal offering of the draught ordeal may be identified with confidence as ergot (Claviceps purpurea), a fungus that infests the grains of barley, wheat, rye, and other cereal grasses."* [9]

---

[9] Merkur, Dan. *The Mystery of Manna: The Psychedelic Sacrament of the Bible*, P. 10.

The woman was poisoned by the draught because she was made to drink the dust, toxic alkaloids and all, along with the water. Had a simple water extraction been performed, sifting out the superfluous and poisonous materials and thereby leaving behind the psychoactive components of the fungus, then the adulterous woman would not have suffered such an ill fate. She would instead have been caught up in an intense and rapturous ecstasy, which was characteristic also of the ingestion of kykeon at the Greater Mystery celebrated at Eleusis.

Significantly, as previously discussed, in the degree of Fellowcraft, the candidate for passing is given a strange word and shown a most peculiar image with little to no meaningful explanation of its presence: *a sheaf of wheat (or ear of corn) suspended near a waterfall.* This depiction is usually found displayed on the south wall of the Lodge, located just behind the Junior Warden. The word associated with it, which can be translated variously as *an ear of corn or a stream of water,* is equally curious. As Pike pointed out,

> *"We do not know when this word was adopted, and no one has ever been able to find any especial significance in it as a Masonic word. But I am entirely satisfied that there was originally a concealed significance in every word used in a Masonic degree. Some secret meaning and application was covered and concealed by each of them."* [10]

To reiterate, Robert Hewitt Brown was likewise suspicious of the traditional explanation provided for the word in question, and in *Stellar Theology and Masonic Astrology* he offered an alternative interpretation, saying that

> *"[a] reference to the Eleusinian Mysteries will go far to clear up [the probable true meaning of 'ears of corn hanging by a water-ford,' or 'a sheaf of wheat suspended near the bank of a river,'] and give us the true import of this symbol."* [11]

And, right he was. The composite meaning of a *shaft of wheat* or *corn*, both known hosts of the ergot fungus, suspended next to or perhaps *beneath* a *waterfall* might be explained by what in modern coffee house parlance has come to be known as a *pour over*, a technique which is used to brew a strong cup of coffee or tea by pouring hot water over the grounds and through a filtration device. If the reader will recall, it is the psychoactive alkaloids of *Claviceps purpurea* which are water soluble, while the poisonous alkaloids are not. Pro-

---

10   Pike, Albert. *The Book of the Words*, P. 47-48.
11   Brown, Robert Hewitt. *Stellar Theology and Masonic Astrology*, P. 155.

THRESHING FLOORS AND WATERFALLS

vided that the wheat or corn in question was infested with the ergot fungus, the act of pouring water over said shafts of wheat or ears of corn would produce a beverage of comparable composition, potency, and effect as the kykeon of Eleusis.

Remarkably, this may also explain another Greek mystery: that of the golden fleece. In *Judges 6:37* the fleece is directly associated with the threshing floor, where Gideon places it there as a curious test from deity. We have already seen that in some cases the threshing floor is code for ergot. Moreover, according to scholars, fleece was actually at one time used by miners near the Black Sea to filter gold flakes out of rivers, making them veritable golden fleeces.[12] If the fleece could filter gold out of a liquid stream, there is no reason it could not have also been used to filter out the harmful components of the ergot fungus. An alternative interpretation of the golden fleece will be offered in a later chapter.

We would like to recall to the reader's attention the fact that to the Eleusinian kykeon was also added pennyroyal mint leaves. In the opinion of Ruck *et al.*, this was included as a means of combating the negative gastric reactions common to ingesting ergot alkaloids. Masonic ritual of course makes no mention of pennyroyal mint leaves, but in a remarkable consistency there is direct mention of multiple gastric aids that would work to much the same advantage as the pennyroyal mint leaves included in the kykeon. We speak here of the so-called symbolic minerals referenced in some versions the Entered Apprentice degree: chalk, charcoal, and clay. Chalk is of course calcium carbonate, the active compound found in digestive aids such as TUMS®. Likewise, charcoal has been long used as a means of treating extreme gastric disturbances and even poisoning. And lastly, clay is the natural source of the anti-diarrheal compound kaolinite, which is a key ingredient in anti-diarrhea medications such as Kaopectate®.

Does this mean that the Greater Mystery of Eleusis has been preserved in the ritual work of Freemasonry? Perhaps that is what the mysterious Alchemist Fulcanelli was alluding to when he cryptically suggested in *The Mystery of the Cathedrals* that the Freemasons expressed themselves in *"argot."*[13] However, to even attempt to answer such a question would be purely speculative. But, then again, so is non-operative Freemasonry.

---

12   Faivre, Antoine. *The Golden Fleece and Alchemy.*
13   Weidner, Jay. *The Mysteries of the Great Cross of Hendaye*, P. 433.

THE VINE OF THE SERPENT

Up until the 1960s, when lysergic acid amides were synthesized from *Ipomoea violacea* and *Turbina corymbosa* seeds by Swiss chemist Dr. Albert Hoffman, the same visionary who discovered the awe-inspiring effects of LSD, it was believed that ergot alkaloids were unique to the ergot fungus alone. Hoffman's remarkable discovery led ethnobotanist Richard Evans Shultes to identify the mysterious *oliloqui* sacrament of the ancient Aztecs, the identity of which had long eluded those before him as being as being part of this same *Convolvulaceae* family.[1] Therefore, the effects of the ergotine *kykeon* potion that was drunk at the celebrated Eleusinian Mysteries would no doubt have been familiar to certain ancient Mesoamericans.

Oliloqui literally means *that which turns*, alluding to the snake-like windings of the vine's tendrils. When consumed, the seeds of the vine induce a powerful LSD-like experience that, according to ethnobotanist Christian Ratsch, is sought out to this day by practitioners of Western sexual magick such as that espoused by British occultist Aleister Crowley.[2] The seeds are traditionally used ceremonially for healing, visionary, and initiatory purposes, and are prepared by being ground into a powder before being combined with water to produce a powerfully inebriating, psychedelic potion. The seeds have also been known to be added in small amounts to alcoholic libations such as mezcal. *Argyreia nervosa* or *Hawaiian Baby Woodrose* seeds, also of the Convolvulaceae family, are known to have been employed toward similar if not identical ends among the Huna shaman of ancient Hawaii. A species of the genus Ipomoea, *jalapa* or *purga*, also features prominently in the African-American folk magic tradition of Hoodoo, where the dried roots of the plant are carried as *High John the Conqueror* amulets.

The formidable effects of oliloqui were noted in the colonial *Florentine Codex* from the 16th century:

> *"It inebriates one; it makes one crazy, stirs one up, makes one mad,*

---
1   Rudgley, Richard. *The Encyclopedia of Psychoactive Substances*, P. 180.
2   Ratsch, Christian. *The Encyclopedia of Psychoactive Plants: Ethnopharmacology and Its Applications*, P. 65.

makes one possessed. He who eats of it, he who drinks of it, sees many things that will make him afraid to a high degree. He is truly terrified of the great snake that he sees for this reason." [3]

Francisco Hernandez, the famous Spanish physician, also discussed oliloqui in his book *Rerum Medicarum Novae Hispaniae Thesarus.*

"When the priests of the indians wish to commune with the spirits of the dead, they eat these seeds to induce a delerium and then see thousands of satanic figures and phantoms around them." [4]

And, after testing the effects of the seeds on human subjects during studies conducted in the early 1990s, research indicated that

"Ingesting 60 - 100 seeds led to apathy, indifference, and increased sensitivity to optical stimuli. After some four hours, there followed a longer-lasting phase of relaxation and well-being." [5]

Having ingested the seeds and experienced much of the above on a number of occasions, we can corroborate these accounts. The effects come on slowly, and the first to be noted is a light-headedness followed by nausea and vomiting. On each occasion, for an hour or longer, we fell into a deep, visionary, death-like trance that was quite Hellish; a veritable Persephone-like descent into the infernal regions of the Underworld. However, following this nightmare-like phase one is reborn into a state of deep and lasting euphoria, paired with visions of geometrical patterns and color. There is a profound sense of the interconnectedness not only of all things; all creation, but also of mind and environment. One has the experience of controlling with the mind his very environment and alternately of losing control of one's mind due the overwhelming intensity of that same environment. For, at times the senses are keyed up to such a degree that phenomena in one's surroundings which would normally go unnoticed are suddenly and simultaneously thrust upon his awareness. The mind is veritably overloaded, and in that moment one can easily give way to panic and confusion. As Aldous Huxley once mused in *The Doors of Perception* in regards to mescaline, under the spell of oliloqui it is as though the reducing valve or funnel which normally would filter out superfluous sensory data from "Mind at Large" and allow one to focus on a single matter has been suddenly

3   TravellersGarden.com
4   American Ethnology Bureau. *Annual Reports*, P. 386.
5   Naturalpedia. *Quotes about apathy from the world's top natural health/natural living authors.*

widened or removed from one's faculties altogether.[6] The final hours of the experience are, for the author, often characterized by what is classically described as *ego death*.

The psychedelic experience cannot be described; not really. The entheogenic realm is the very thing to which the phrase *ineffable mysteries* refers. The ineffable mysteries cannot be shared or even comprehended in their fullness except by one has obtained *gnosis* from experiencing those mysteries directly. Such a person was called in the Eleusinian Mysteries an *Epopt* or *Seer*, and the corresponding injunction of secrecy in the Mysteries likely alludes to the very real inability on the part of the Epopt to communicate the experience successfully.

Where the Eleusinian Mysteries have not been practiced as such for some two thousand years, there exists to this day certain Mesoamericans who employ ergotine alkaloids to similar ends. While modern day Freemasonry has no demonstrable ties to the ancient Aztecs, their culture is one to which we might look in order to better understand the potential role of ergot in the mysteries celebrated at Eleusis as well as perhaps in Freemasonry, where, the secret of the ergot fungus appears to have been symbolically preserved in the form of a threshing floor, a mysterious password, and an allegorical sheaf of wheat suspended next to a waterfall.

---

[6] Fietz, Lothar. *Aldous Huxley: Pratexte und Kontexte*, P. 77

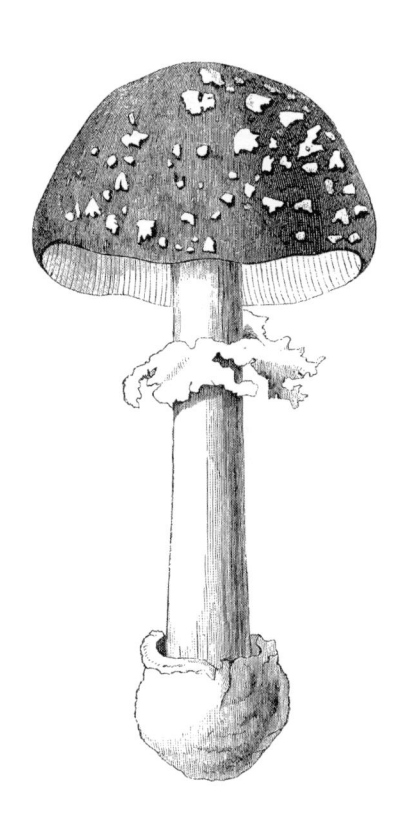

PART III: FLY AGARIC

MASONIC TEMPLARY, GUARDIANS OF THE GRAIL

Ever since the early to mid-thirteenth century, when German knight Wolfram von Eschenbach identified them as such in his epic poem *Parzival*, the legendary Knights Templar have been closely associated with the mythical Knights of the Holy Grail. In the paragraphs which follow it will be demonstrated that Von Eschenbach's association may have influenced the development of the Templar knighting ceremony in the York Rite and the Knight Kadosh degree in the Ancient and Accepted Scottish Rite. It is on this account that the author has come to view Masonic Templary as something of a modern guardian of the authentic Grail tradition.

Let us take a moment to briefly touch upon some of what it is that the Grail tradition actually entails. It will also be helpful to examine a couple of the primary literary precursors which some scholars believe may have contributed to the rich lore surrounding the Grail tradition. The Holy Grail is most commonly depicted as being the cup from which Jesus Christ drank during his 'Last Supper' prior to being crucified. According to legend, this cup was later used by Joseph of Arimathea[1], to collect the mixture of blood and water which flowed from the laceration in Jesus' side made by the lance or spear of Roman soldier Longinus. Being thus sanctified, the cup was then said to have been imbued with miraculous virtues such as curative powers and the ability to make barren land fertile, and it was for the purpose of preserving this sacred vessel that the Order of the Knights of the Holy Grail was originally founded.

As a literary precursor to this tale, several scholars have sought to identify the legend of the Holy Grail with the Welsh legend of King Bran, the mythical king of Britain, and his magical cauldron – the latter of which was said, similar to the qualities attributed to the Holy Grail, to be able to mysteriously restore the dead to life. Magical characteristics such as these were not limited to King Bran's cauldron, but were also attributed to Bran himself.[2] According to

---
1   The secret disciple of Christ who donated the tomb wherein Christ was to be laid following his crucifixion.
2   Dom, David. *King Arthur and the Gods of the Round Table*, P. 131.

The Mabinogi, an ancient book of Welsh folklore, after realizing his impending fate, the king ordered that his head be severed and returned to Britain where, like the singing severed head of the poet Orpheus, it continued to speak and, in some cases, even prophesize. After some eighty years, however, the head ceased speaking, at which time it was taken to a place called 'White Hill' and buried facing the direction of France in order to protect the British from French invasion. The legend even goes on to declare that it was none other than King Arthur, the same who features prominently in the Grail tradition, who recovered the skull from its place of rest.

In more recent times, scholars have sought to align the Holy Grail with the golden platter on which the severed head of St. John the Baptist was served to the dancing Salome by the remorseful King Herod.[3] The reader is asked to note that in both cases the object identified as a forerunner of the Holy Grail is directly associated with the motif of a severed head.

The Knights Templar were formed in the 12th century for the noble purpose of escorting Christians on their pilgrimages throughout the Holy Land during the Crusades. After inventing a system that is widely recognized as the forerunner of modern banking, the Templars grew exceedingly wealthy to the point that the powers that be; that is, the crown and the tiara, sought to relieve them of their riches, and in 1307 a statement was issued by the debt-ridden King Philip IV of France declaring the Templars to be heretics. A great many of them were subsequently arrested, interrogated, tortured, and executed – their wealth then claimed by the greedy Philip. While no 'holy cup' was reported to have ever been discovered amongst the Templars' treasures, the most widespread of the confessions made by the knights during their interrogation was the collective veneration of a mysterious severed head, reportedly called Baphomet, which was used by them during their ceremonies of initiation.

According to nineteenth century Viennese Orientalist Joseph von Hammer-Purgstall – who believed that Baphomet was not the name of a deity but rather the title of a secret Ophite Gnostic initiation ritual – the word Baphomet is a combination of the two Greek words *Baphe* and *Metis* which, when combined, translates to the *Baptism of Wisdom*.[4] Of course, this may have been less of literal and more of a metaphorical baptism. Although, it is perhaps notable that Von Eschenbach specifically refers to the Knights of the Holy Grail as "baptized men."

As stated, the lore surrounding the Grail tradition is intimately connected with legends involving severed heads. These two seemingly separate themes, a sacred cup and a severed head, would appear somewhat irreconcilable if it

---

[3] Picknett, Lynn. *The Templar Revelation: Secret Guardians of the True Identity of Christ*, P. 137.

[4] Twyman, Tracy R. *Found Again: The "Templar Artifacts" of Hammer-Purgstall*.

was not for two Masonic degrees styled *Templar*. In both the Knight Templar ceremony in the York Rite and the Knight Kadosh degree in the Ancient and Accepted Scottish Rite, Southern Jurisdiction, the candidate is made to seal his obligation by drinking wine from the cap of a human skull, thus uniting neatly the theme of the sacred cup or libation with that of the skull or severed head. This practice, though, is not unique to Freemasonry. We find a historical precedent in the potentially shocking rituals once observed by the Goths of Scandinavia who, according to the research of English Freemason Rev. George Oliver, were prone to drink alcoholic libations from the cap of a human skull. Paraphrasing from Oliver's 1840 work *The History of Initiation*, Albert Pike says in *Morals and Dogma* that the initiatory rituals of this Eastern Germanic tribe included

> "[a] long probation, of fasting and mortification, circular processions, [and] many fearful tests and trials...[The candidate] was obligated upon a naked sword (as is still the custom in the Rit Moderne), and sealed his obligation by drinking mead out of a human skull." [5]

Turning our attention to the Far East, we find that the ritual motif of drinking from a human skull also plays a central role in the ceremonial observances of the reclusive Shiva worshipping *Aghora* of India, as well as the remote *Vajrayana Buddhists* of Tibet, both of whom preserve the curious rite of imbibing libations from a sacred *kapala* or skullcup. These kapalas are often employed by the practitioners of Vajrayana Buddhism for the additional purpose of making religious offerings to the deific *Dharmapalas*, who themselves are frequently depicted as bearing these strange yet fascinating relics. The word *Dharmapala* literally translated means *Defender of the Faith*, which itself is a phrase that should be particularly meaningful to every Masonic Templar. However, they're also employed in Tantric empowerments, during which, according to Kagyu lay lama Mike Crowley, the kapala is regularly filled with one or more inebriants.

Frederick Shade, in his *The Quest for the Holy Grail and the Modern Knights Templar*, provides an outline of several other similarities between what he calls the Templar hallows and the lesser hallows of the Grail tradition. The lesser hallows of the Grail tradition are described as being certain sacred relics for which the Grail Knights are searching in addition to the Holy Grail. The similarities between the so-called Templar hallows and the lesser hallows of the Grail tradition include, among other things

---

5   De Hoyos, Arturo. *Albert Pike's Morals and Dogma: Annotated Edition*, P. 509-510.

> "[t]he dish of bread, which is the food given to the pilgrim on his arrival" and "[t]he skull of mortality, with which the novice undertakes a year of penance, and with which the imprecations are made."[6]

Shade goes on to say that

> "[t]here are several other hallows and sacred signs in the Templar tradition. Some of the lesser hallows of the Grail cycle are suggested here, such as the Templar crucifix, with the nails prominently displayed thereon. There is the knight's sword, which is to be wielded in defense of the faith and also his shield, all which are beautifully explained in the quotation from St. Paul. They may not necessarily come directly from the Grail legend, but they certainly evoke many aspects of that tradition and resonate as hallows in their own right."[7]

Von Eschenbach's association of the Knights Templar with the mythical Knights of the Holy Grail may very well have had more than a minor influence on the development of the Templar knighting ceremony in the York Rite and the Knight Kadosh degree in the AASR. Because of the probability of said influence, it is the author's opinion that Masonic Templary can rightly be called a modern guardian of the authentic Grail tradition, furnished with all that such entails. This is true for the candidate who sits silently contemplating in the grim Chamber of Reflections at the commencement of the Templar ceremony, where the human skull present there still has the potential to exhibit that miraculous power of prophetic speech attributed to the severed head of the mythical King Bran. Surrounded oftentimes with oracular messages such as *I was what you are* and, more importantly, *I am what you will be*, does not the skull in the Chamber of Reflections speak something of our fate to us all? Is not the bitter cup of death that from which every man must sooner or later partake?

---

6   Shade, Frederick, A. *The Quest for the Holy Grail and the Modern Knights Templar.*
7   *Ibid.*

BAPHOMET AND THE GOLDEN FLEECE

Baphomet, the alleged deific icon of the Knights Templar, has remained something of an enigma to scholars for centuries. The figure was described by some as having been a mysterious severed head which was possessive of magical qualities. However, the most well-known depiction of *Baphomet* comes from French occultist and Freemason Eliphas Levi's sketch of the same in his highly influential work *The Dogma and Ritual of High Magic*.[1] In said book, *Baphomet* is depicted as being a winged, hermaphroditic hominid with the head and legs of a goat, but having the torso of a man. It was established in the previous chapter that the name of *Baphomet* was in all probability a coded reference to an Ophite Gnostic-turn-Templar initiatory ritual wherein was made use of a sacred *grail* of libation, the same having been fashioned from the skullcap of a severed head; that is, a *kapala* or *skull-cup*. The precedent for such a rite has been set by ritual observances throughout the occident and orient alike. So, why then was Eliphas Levi, an occultist of no small amount of learning, apt to depict the figure as being related to a goat? Was Levi simply confused? Or was he employing a *blind* for the purpose of misdirecting profane eyes? These are the questions which will be treated in the paragraphs below.

We explained in the previous chapter, the name *Baphomet* is assuredly a combination of the two Greek words *Baphe* and *Metis* which, when translated into English, yields the phrase *Baptism of Wisdom*.[2] The *Baphomet* skull venerated by the Knights Templar has been variously identified as the head of Bran, the mythical king of Britain, and more significantly, the head of John the Baptist, the initiator of Christ. In the present chapter, we will examine yet another possible candidate for the historical, literary validation of our cherished skull-grail: the head of the Gorgon Medusa. But, before we get to that, let us take a moment look at still another famous skull that was said to have been in the possession of the historical Knights Templar.

In his 1921 work *Freemasonry and the Ancient Gods*, J.S.M. Ward,

---

1   Levi, Eliphas. *Transcendental Magic: Its Doctrine and Ritual*, P. 180.
2   Twyman, Tracy R. *Found Again: The "Templar Artifacts" of Hammer-Purgstall*.

the founder of the *Anthropological School* of Masonic research, recounted a disturbing yet fascinating tale that has allegedly come down to us from the very trials of the historical Templars. While the story is a fiction which was concocted in an attempt to slander the Knights of the Temple, it is not without pertinence regarding our task at hand. According to Ward,

> *"[a] great lady of Maraclea was loved by a Templar, a Lord of Sidon; but she died in her youth, and on the night of her burial this wicked lover crept to the grave, dug up her body, and violated it. Then a voice from the void bade him return in nine months' time, for he would find a son. He obeyed the injunction, and at the appointed time opened the grave again and found a head on the leg bones of a skeleton (skull and cross-bones). The same voice bade him 'guard it well, for it would be the giver of all good things,' and so he carried it away with him. It became a protecting genius, and he was able to defeat his enemies by merely showing them the magic head."* [3]

Drawing from this account, Carl A.P. Ruck and his co-authors Mark A. Hoffman and Jose Alfredo Gonzalez Celdran added that

> *"The Knights Templar adopted the Crux decussata as their flag and emblem. They depicted it as crossed leg bones, beneath a skull, supposedly as a reference to Golgotha, the Hill of Skulls, but perhaps not without knowledge of the [Gorgon head]...This is especially likely because in Templar lore the skull [was used] as a magical weapon, just as Perseus used the Gorgon head."* [4]

It is this amazingly perceptive injunction on the part of Ruck, Hoffman, and Celdran which provides the key to understanding precisely what is being implied by the name and essential nature of *Baphomet*.

According to myth, Perseus was the first of the Greek heroes and was the legendary founder of the city of Mycenae. In order to win his bride Andromeda, Perseus was charged with the impossible task of recovering the head of the Gorgon Medusa who, like our own *Baphomet*, was described as being part human and part beast; in this case, half serpent. Perseus' quest for the Gorgon head has been rightly associated by scholars with Herakles' search for

---

3   Ward, J.S.M. *Freemasonry and the Ancient Gods*, P. 307.
4   Ruck, Carl A.P. *Mushrooms, Myth and Mithras: The Drug Cult that Civilized Europe*, P. 212.

the Golden Apples of the Hersperides and, more importantly, Jason's quest for the Golden Fleece. In each of these cases, the prize was finally discovered in a serpent-guarded tree amidst a sacred garden or grove.

The version of the Perseus' ordeal with which most are familiar describes his confrontation with Medusa as having taken place in the Gorgon's cave, located far beyond the lair of the Granae sisterhood. However, other accounts place the Gorgon Medusa in the very Garden of the Hesperides, the same local where Herakles discovered the Golden Apples. An example of this stream of transmission was preserved and can be seen depicted on a Greek vase housed at the Staatliche Museum in Berlin, Germany, which has been dated back to third quarter of the fourth century, BC. This amazing artifact features the hero Perseus as standing directly beneath the Golden Apple tree in the Garden of the Hesperides. Before him is seated a decapitated Gorgon Medusa, while the victorious Perseus bears her severed head. In the painting, however, the eyes of Perseus are not directed toward the Gorgon or her head, but instead are aimed solely at the golden fruit dangling from the tree, thereby subtly identifying for the viewer the Gorgon head with the Golden Apples. It may therefore be safely assumed that the head of Medusa, the Golden Apples (*mela*), and the Golden Fleece (*mela*) are all three synonymous. Indeed, *mela* translates to both *apple* and *fleece*.

So, aside from the inherent notions of an epic quest, what have these to do with the *Holy Grail* and thus with *Baphomet*? According to the 6th century chronographer John Malalas,

> "Perseus cut off [Medusa's] head and then used it as a 'skull-cup' (skyphos) to teach the rite of Zoroaster [i.e., the haoma rite] to the Persians, who took the name of Medes (Medoi) in honor of the Medusa."[5]

Just as in the Knight Templar ceremony in the York Rite and the Knight Kadosh degree in the AASR, a libation imbibed via a cup fashioned from a skull is employed. And, the similarities do not stop there. Both versions of the story report that Perseus was aided in his task by Athena, the goddess of Wisdom, who told him how to defeat Medusa. Following Perseus' victory, the Gorgon head was therefore entrusted to Athena as a gift. From thenceforth she employed the *skyphos* or "skull-cup" as a decorative broach to fasten her goatskin *aegis*, which is considered by many to be the wise goddess' defining characteristic.

In modern parlance, the word *aegis* has come to suggest the *covering* of protection offered to a worshipper by a given deity. The word itself, however,

---

5   *Ibid*, P. 88-89.

simply means *goatskin*. The association between the Gorgon skull-cup and the hide of a goat points of course directly back to *Baphomet* which, if the reader will recall, was depicted by Levi as being part goat. And here we approach the real mystery of the myth. According to Ruck and Heinrich's *The Apples of Apollo*,

> *"The magical item that was the object of the hero's quest in Greek mythology is always the sacred entheogen. In the case of Jason, the Golden Fleece was ultimately Amanita muscaria. …As should be apparent by now…the fleece [and] apples…represent the fly-agaric mushroom. …[Carefully]-dried fly-agaric caps turn a metallic golden-orange color. This is the reason why both the magic fleece and the magic apples are called 'golden.' What may be less apparent is why the mushroom should be compared to a fleece, or an apple, golden or otherwise.*
>
> *In its ovoid embryonic stage, the fly-agaric is completely covered by a pure white membrane called the universal veil. The portion of the veil that covers the nascent cap is comprised of contiguous pointed segments, the purpose of which is to protect the cap and, by insinuating these 'horns' into tiny cracks in the covering soil, aid the mushroom in breaking through to the air. As the mushroom cap grows and expands, the segments separate and are spread apart, giving the opened red cap its characteristic white-spotted appearance. Looked at closely, these veil fragments, sometimes up to a quarter-inch high and wide, resemble white wool, especially to those of a pastoral society. The blood-red 'skin' of the cap heightens the illusion.*
>
> *When harvested, the cap of the mushroom is usually severed from the stalk to prevent infestation from fly larvae often found there. …The separated cap is then dried, both to prevent infestation and rot and to make the mushroom a more potent entheogen, for drying converts ibotenic acid to the much more effective muscimol.*
>
> *Several other changes occur as well. As the cap dries, it deflates, shrinks in overall size, and wrinkles; as mentioned, it also turns a beautiful golden color with a metallic sheen, or a tawny orange if handled carelessly. Caps will always re-absorb a little moisture from the air after drying, giving them a suppleness and feel similar to cures animal hides, which they now resemble: they look and feel*

like the hides of tiny animals. If you ever have seen such 'hides,' the 'Golden Fleece'…suddenly [comes] into focus.

The fly-agaric is a mycorrhizal fungus; that is, its mycelium will only grow in association with the rootlets of certain trees. Because of this, the fruiting bodies of Amanita muscaria mycelia, the red and white mushrooms themselves, will always pop their round white-spotted heads into view beneath the canopy of their host, giving the impression that they are ripe fruit that has fallen from the tree. Because they are round and red and the proper size, they are likened to apples by anyone familiar with that fruit. And again, because they turn golden as they dry, they therefore become golden apples.

Golden Fleece and Golden Apples: only, and always, found in certain special 'gardens,' on certain special trees." [6]

It takes no great leap of speculation to imagine that the golden fleece for which Jason was searching, the same of which was later 'fastened' with the Gorgon skull cup, is in reference to this same animal hide *covering*. It is therefore possible, dare I say probable, that the Holy Grail and the golden fleece are indeed implicative of the same mystery; that is, of the mushroom. Moreover, the mother of Athena was none other than the goddess Metis. It very nearly goes without saying that this would appear to be the source of the latter half of the name of *Baphomet*; that is, *Baphe* **Metis**. Interestingly, *Metis* is also an important philosophical concept. According to Amy Wygant,

"Metis as a quality refers to practical ability, craft, magic, herbs… and resourcefulness of every kind." [7]

The relation of Metis to practical magic and the use of herbs is particularly notable.

It is apparent that Levi's curious association of *Baphomet* with the goat is no mere confusion of symbols, but rather a veritable covering, serving to obscure the *Arcana* by yet another *blind*. Moreover, the man was not ignorant of the use of entheogenic plants. For example, he says in *The History of Magic by Eliphas Levi:*

6   Ruck, Carl A.P. *The Apples of Apollo: Pagan and Christian Mysteries of the Eucharist*, P. 118-119.
7   Wygant, Amy. *Medea, Magic, and Modernity in France: Stages and Histories*, 1553 – 1797, P. 57

> *"The progress of Magnetism will one day lead to the discovery of the absorbent properties of the Mistletoe of the Oak. We shall then know the secret of those spongy excrescences which draw their unused surplus from trees, and surcharge themselves from their tinctures and sap; the Mushrooms, the Truffles, the Galls of trees... Then we will no more laugh at Paracelsus..."* [8]

Of course, the oak tree is a common host to the mycorrhizal fungus *fly agaric*. The reference to Paracelsus is telling, too, as the Alchemistic healer actually refers to an *agaric* in his writings.[9]

Again, in A.E. Waite's *The Mysteries of Magic: A Digest of the Writings of Eliphas Levi* (1886) we read:

> *"In the middle ages, the necromancers...compounded philtres and ointments...; they mixed aconite, belladonna, and poisonous fungi... Their howlings were heard at great distances, and the belated traveler fancied that legions of phantoms were issuing from the earth; the very trees assumed in his eyes affrighting shapes, flaming orbs seemed glaring in the thickets, while frogs of the marshes appeared to repeat hoarsely the words of the Sabbath. It was the mesmerism of hallucination and the contagion of madness. [They] extracted the poisonous and narcotic humour from fungi."* [10]

Replete with aural and visual hallucinations, morphing, menacing phantasms, disembodied orbs of light, and even frogs chanting the liturgy of the Orthodox Church, Levi's account is clearly an example of entheogenic intoxication.

Similar to the Holy Grail in Von Eschenbach's *Parzival*, the Templar's *Baptism of Wisdom* has been thickly veiled from the eyes of the profane, so much so that it has even become something of a mystery even to Masonry's own Initiates. It is the author's hope that he has been at least somewhat successful in his attempt to demonstrate these more than subtle connections between such apparently disparate themes as the Holy Grail, a severed head, and the golden fleece. While it is true that the quest for truth oftentimes takes on multiple forms and themes, the underlying object has and will always remain the same: the golden light of Wisdom.

---

8   Waite, Arthur Edward. *The History of Magic by Eliphas Levi*, P. 185.
9   Weeks, Andrew. *Paracelsus (Theophrastus Bombastus Von Hohenheim, 1493-1541): Essential Theoretical Writings*, P. 32.
10   Waite, Arthur Edward. *The Mysteries of Magic: A Digest of the Writings of Eliphas Levi*, pp.135-174.

THE HOLY GRAIL AND SOMA

We have demonstrated that the Holy Grail of Arthurian legend was assuredly a veiled allusion to *Baphomet*, the mysterious severed head allegedly venerated by the original Knights Templar. It was further demonstrated that Masonic Templary in turn incorporated this imagery into its own ritual in the form of an initiatory skull cup, the same of which fulfills the requirements of being both a severed head and a sacred cup. In the present chapter we will tackle the problem of the contents of this cup and discover what it was exactly, aside from its composition and legendary history, that made this particular vessel so very special. To do this we will first need to turn again to the East and look as far back as 1500BCE. For, it is there that we will find the *Vedas* and, more importantly, *soma*.

To this day soma is surrounded by mystery. It is spoken of in the *Vedas* as being at once a plant, a libation, a drug, a bull, and even a deity. Known most commonly as the 'Red Bull' and often described as having but a single leg and foot, soma is not unlike the famed fruit of the tree of life in Judeo Christian lore or the legendary *amrita* of the Hindus or *ambrosia* of the Greeks. Like them, it was purported to confer upon its drinker the gift of immortality. However, soma's identification has eluded scholars for centuries, and it was not until the arrival on the scene of amateur mycologist R. Gordon Wasson that a reasonable proposal was set forth, which satisfies most if not all of the requirements detailed in the Vedas.

Wasson identified soma as the entheogenic and mycorrhizal *Amanita muscaria* mushroom, commonly known as *fly agaric* and still widely used today for ritualistic and religious purposes by numerous indigenous peoples including the shaman of Siberia. Without entering into the difficult question of whether or not Wasson was correct in his identification (which we believe he was), the reader is directed to his books *Soma: the Divine Mushroom of Immortality* and *Persephone's Quest: Entheogens and the Origins of Religion* for a full treatment of the subject.[1]

---

1   In his book *Cannabis and the Soma Solution*, Chris Bennett has argued convincingly that soma was actually *Cannabis sativa*. It is our suspicion that both he and Wasson are correct, and soma very likely answered to different plants at different epochs.

As stated above, *A. muscaria* mushrooms are entheogenic or psychedelic and contain within them a powerful visionary and intoxicating compound called muscimol. When properly prepared and ingested at a safe dosage by humans these mushrooms have the potential to induce visions of light and sensations of ascension and dissolution, as well as cause profound introspection and revelations of a personal as well as cosmic nature. On the flip side, they can also induce terrifying hallucinations, disorientation, distortions of time and space, flushing, extreme perspiration, and brutal nausea.

Clark Heinrich explains in his remarkable book *Strange Fruit* that the *A. muscaria* mushroom begins its life as a small, egg shaped mass before expanding on its stipe into a platter-like cap and finally into its matured chalice shape. Its 'red with white spots' appearance is familiar to us all as the so-called fairytale mushroom seen in popular children's stories such as Lewis Carroll's *Alice In Wonderland*. The white spots are the remnants of the universal veil, which serves two important purposes. Firstly, it protects the fruiting body before the mushroom has had time to expand its bright red cap. Secondly, with its numerous small points, like several tiny horns, the universal veil assists the fruiting body in reaching the sunlight by breaking up any soil which might cover it. Hence soma's being likened unto a 'red bull' in the Vedas. The epithet of single foot therefore refers of course to the lone stipe which supports the ruddy cap. This figurative bull had to be slain by the worshippers via pressing out its rich, intoxicating blood. Indeed, soma even means pressed one. According to the Vedas, the juices of the Red Bull would be pressed out between two stones and mixed with cow's milk before being ritually drunk by the congregation of worshippers.

It is believed that soma eventually became exclusive to the Brahmin priesthood and its use by those of other castes was deemed taboo. One early Hindu law maker, Manu, even went so far as to declare that the consumption of mushrooms be outlawed completely. Soma did not disappear from view altogether, however. As many scholars have pointed out, it survived with the ancient Hindus' Middle Eastern neighbors, the Zoroastrians, under the name of *haoma*. Like soma, haoma is described at once as a plant and a libation, as well as a bull, and is even mentioned in the Zoroastrian holy book the Zend-Avesta.

In the previous chapter it was explained that, according to the ancient Greek legend, after decapitating the Gorgon, Perseus used Medusa's head as a "skull-cup" to "teach the rite of Zoroaster to the Persians, the same of whom took the name of Medes in honor of the Medusa." Medea is of course where Zoroaster, the founder of the Zoroastrian religion, is said to have been born. According to scholars, a similar tradition was preserved by the eleventh-century Byzantine historian Greogorios Kedrenos, who claimed that Perseus, after bringing it to earth, deposited the celestial fire in a sacred temple and instructed the priesthood in the mystical rites of initiation. In this way, Kedrenos says, the haoma-using priesthood of the Magi was instituted.

As Carl A.P. Ruck has observed, it is no coincidence that most scholars agree; the sound which the Gorgon sisterhood made was a mooing. That is, "the lowing of cattle was their sound." Not unlike with soma and haoma, the Gorgon from which the skull cup came is implicitly associated with cattle. It is also notable that here we have our first example of the contents of the cup as being consubstantial with its vessel; that is, both the skull cup and its contents allude to the mushroom. Indeed, for 'skull cap' is even a name commonly applied by laymen to mushrooms of various species.

It was during their travels in the Middle East that Roman soldiers are suspected to have first encountered the haoma rite, which they then established in their own homeland in the form of the Mithraic Mysteries. Known as Mithra to the Zoroastrians, Mithras also appears in the Vedas as Mitra, an epithet of soma which means a friend of man. Conveniently, Mithras is also known as the 'lord of cattle pastures,' keeping with our peculiar but prevalent bovine theme. Mithra's role in the Zoroastrian religion was as divine mediator. However, the role he played in the Roman manifestation of his cult was considerably more complex.

The Roman cult of Mithras was for all practical purposes a secret society composed almost wholly of Roman soldiers. Specifically, they were holy warriors. Similar to Freemasonry, the Mithraic Mysteries consisted of a hierarchical structure of initiatory degrees or levels of attainment wherein the mysteries of the cult were progressively imparted to the initiate as he made his advancement through the grades. The final grade, that of *Pater* or *Father*, was symbolized by what appears to be a bowl and staff, suggestive of the cap and stipe of a mushroom, depicted next to a ruddy and spotted Phrygian cap, also known as a skull cap – and equally indicative of the mushroom – and next to that, a pruning hook, not unlike the one used by Perseus to decapitate Medusa before using the cap of her skull to teach the haoma rite to the Persians. The members of the Mithraic cult met in small subterranean chambers called Mithraea that were cave-like in appearance. Similar to a Masonic Lodge, the floors of the Mithraea were consistently designed as a rectangle or oblong square. Quite unlike a Masonic Lodge, on the other hand, is the fact that the eastern wall of every Mithraeum included a depiction of the *Tauroctony*, a fresco or relief which featured a Mithras clad in red with white spots, supported on one leg like the 'single-footed' soma and donning a Phrygian cap (also known as a 'liberty cap'), and triumphing over a sacred bull. Here, as with the *A. muscaria* consuming shaman of Siberia, Mithras has made himself consubstantial with the mushroom, taking on the appearance of the object of sacrifice. Furthermore, the shape of the single leg on which Mithras supports himself, paired with the suggestive folds of his clothing and armor in that region, very much itself resembles the cap and stipe of a fruiting body.

The Phrygian cap worn by Mithras is no doubt familiar to members of the Southern Jurisdiction of the Ancient and Accepted Scottish Rite where, in the Knights Kadosh degree (the Knights Kadosh naturally being the Knights Templar), one encounters the suggestive Liberty Pole in the form of a Phrygian cap placed atop a shepherd's crook. Note that in addition to the fact that the liberty pole and liberty cap are both common euphemisms for various mushrooms, the Knights Kadosh degree, just like the Templar ceremony in the York Rite, is the degree wherein the candidate drinks from a skull cup.

Rosicrucian scholar Hargrave Jennings tells us in his book *The Rosicrucians: Their Rites and Mysteries* that

> *"the real meaning of the... 'cap of liberty' has been involved from time immemorial in deep obscurity, notwithstanding that it has always been regarded as a most important hieroglyph.... It signifies the supernatural simultaneous 'sacrifice' and 'triumph.' ...The whole is a sign of 'initiation,' and of baptism of a peculiar kind."* [2]

It is here that we come full circle back to that other secret society of holy warriors with whom we first began: the Knights Templar. As was explained in our previous treatments, in his epic poem *Perzival* knight Wolfram von Eschenbach identified the Grail Knights of Arthurian legend as the Knights Templar. During their fateful trial we know that many of the Templars confessed to the veneration a mysterious severed head, named by some as Baphomet. It is quite possible that the Templars, like their Roman predecessors in the Mithraic Mysteries, employed the *A. muscaria* mushroom in an initiatory context, and that this mysterious severed head was actually no more than the symbolic vessel; a *kapala* or skull cup, consubstantial with its contents, with which the soma or haoma was ritually drunk. After all, as Von Hammer demonstrated, Baphomet is not the name of an elusive deity. Rather, it is the description of a sacred and secret ritual act employed by the Templars in an initiatory context: *Baphe Metis*, the 'Baptism of Wisdom.' It is notable that Apollonios of Tyana is actually known to have traveled to the India where he reportedly was physically baptized with the soma sacrament of the Vedic religion by the Brahmans themselves. A "baptism of a peculiar kind" indeed.

However, unlike our previous subjects, neither the Knights Templar nor the Grail Knights are associated with any sort of bovine symbolism. Still, as Heinrich ably demonstrates, there is no better candidate for the Holy Grail than the *Amanita muscaria* mushroom. Indeed, for the grail is found precisely

---

[2] Jennings, Hargrave. *The Rosicrucians: Their Rites and Mysteries*, P. 274.

where one would expect to find *A. muscaria* mushrooms, in the forest. For, as stated above, *A. muscaria* is a mycorrhizal mushroom, meaning that it can only be found growing within and upon the root systems of host trees. It is quite literally the fruit of the roots of the trees whereon it is found. And, like *A. muscaria*, depending on the version of the story, the grail is described variously as a stone, a platter, and a cup. Recall that the life cycle of *A. muscaria* progresses from its egg or 'stone' shape to that of a flat platter on a stipe, and thence to that of a chalice.

In the Arthurian legends the grail is identified as the cup which Jesus used at the so-called last supper; a cup which was later used by Joseph of Arimathea to collect the blood issuing from the wound in Jesus' side during his crucifixion. The Knight Templar ceremony, on the other hand, names the grail or skull cup as the *bitter cup of death*, thereby directly aligning it with the cup from which Jesus drank at Gethesmane.

> *"We know from the canonical book of Mark that a fifth person was with Jesus, Peter, James, and John at Gethesmane after the [last supper]... Here is one possible scenario. Everyone at the supper took two forms of the mushroom, the 'bread' [the dried mushroom cap] and the 'wine' [the 'soma']. Jesus had arranged to initiate a young man afterwards at Gethesmane. Meeting the youth at the garden, Jesus posted his three most trusted disciples as guards so the secret rite wouldn't be disturbed. Jesus went off with the young man, who was naked except for a linen cloth around his body, to initiate him into the mysteries of the kingdom of God."* [3]

When Jesus said, "Take away this cup from me."[4], was he initiating his followers with a *Baptism of Wisdom*? More will be offered on the Christian connection in the following chapter.

It should be noted that *A. muscaria* has been used by at least one Masonic order. According to Rene Le Forestier, the incense blend used by Martinez de Pasqually and his order Elus Cohens[5] included "spore of agaric."[6] While the spores of *A. muscaria* are not psychoactive, the fact that the mushroom is referenced at all is worthy of mention. Even Rev. William Alexander Ayton, the famed Alchemist of the Hermetic Order of the Golden Dawn, purported

---
[3]   Heinrich, Clark. *Strange Fruit: Alchemy and Religion, the Hidden Truth*, P. 108.
[4]   *The Holy Bible, KJV*, Mark 14:36
[5]   The Elus Cohen was the first real high grade system of Freemasonry. Essentially theurgic in nature, the Elus Cohen was the ultimate source for both Louis Claude de Saint-Martin's system Martinism, officially organized by Papus as the Martinist Order, and Jean-Baptiste Willermoz' system CBCS, the apex of the Rectified Scottish Rite.
[6]   McIntosh, Christopher. *Eliphas Levi and the French Occult Revival*, P. 21-25.

THE HOLY GRAIL AND SOMA 91

to have received and drank the "real Soma juice", upon his initiation into the Hermetic Brotherhood of Luxor.[7] In fact, soma is spoken of too by the infamous H.P. Blavatsky in her book *The Secret Doctrine*:

> "But the real property of the true Soma was (and is) to make a new man of the Initiate, after he is reborn, namely once that he begins to live in his astral body ...The partaker of Soma finds himself both linked to his external body, and yet away from it in his spiritual form. The latter, freed from the former, soars for the time being in the ethereal higher regions, becoming virtually 'as one of the gods,' and yet preserving in his physical brain the memory of what he sees and learns. Plainly speaking, Soma is the fruit of the Tree of Knowledge forbidden by the jealous Elohim to Adam and Eve or Yah-ve, 'lest Man should become as one of us.'"[8]

We close this section with a quote from Freemason and Sufi Rene Guenon.

> "[Concerning Lost Words and Substituted Words, an] example... can be found notably in the Mazdean tradition, and in this connection we should add that what was lost is represented not only by the sacred cup, that is, by the Grail or various of its equivalents, but also by what it contains. This is readily enough understood, for the content, however designated, is actually nothing other than the 'draught of immortality,' the possession of which essentially constitutes one of the privilages of the primordial state. Thus it is said that after the Vedic soma became unknown in a certain epoch, it was necessary to substitute another draught that only represented it; and although not positively indicated anywhere, it even seems that this substitute was later lost in turn. ...And while on this subject it bears recalling that in other traditions wine also substitutes for the 'draught of immortality,' moreover, this is why it is generally taken as a symbol of the hidden or guarded doctrine, namely, esoteric and initiatic knowledge..."[9]

---

7   Godwin, Joscelyn. *The Hermetic Brotherhood of Luxor: Initiatic and Historical Documents of an Order of Practical Occultism*, P. 75.
8   Blavatsky, H.P. *The Secret Doctrine: The Synthesis of Science, Religion, and Philosophy.*, Vol. II, P. 499.
9   Guenon, Rene. *Studies in Freemasonry and the Compagnonnage*, P. 20-21.

THE CHRISTIAN CONNECTION

If the Holy Grail was indeed an allusion to the *Amanita muscaria* mushroom, then why the traditional association of the grail with Jesus and the early Christian religion? Enter archaeologist John M. Allegro. Allegro was one of the scholars responsible for translating the famed *Dead Sea Scrolls*, but his claim to infamy was a curious little book titled *The Sacred Mushroom and the Cross*. In it, Allegro argued per etymological indicators that the early Christian religion was nothing short of a fertility and mushroom cult, and that Jesus, who likely did not exist, was either a symbolic representative of the mushroom itself or of its resultant effects. This line of argument has been ably continued by more recent scholars such as Clark Heinrich and Carl A.P. Ruck.

The first indication of fungus in the Jesus story appears when he does; with his birth. We are told in the New Testament that this event was accompanied by the visitation of three wise men or, to be more specific, three *Magi*. The Magi were the priests of the ancient Mazdean religion. As we saw earlier, the Mazdean religion continued the Vedic soma sacrament in the form of haoma before influencing the Roman cult of Mithras and ultimately Christianity. This portion of the Jesus story therefore has direct connotations to the fly agaric mushroom.

Another fungal indicator is the miracle worked at the wedding party where, after the supply of wine had been exhausted, Jesus took to turning ordinary water into a powerful wine. *Soma* of course means *pressed one*, indicating its method of preparation; *i.e.*, it is pressed in, and its essence infused with, water. This creates a powerful, fragrant potion that, like wine, is both deep red and thoroughly intoxicating. Recall that, perhaps significantly, at both David's threshing floor and at the garden of Gethesmane a *winepress* was present.

The wine which Jesus reportedly made was specifically noted as being "good" wine; that is, it was stronger and better than the wine which they had already depleted. Prior the discovery of alcohol distillation in the 16th century, all wines would have been more or less the same potency. Fermentation alone will only yield an ABV of roughly 13-18%. But, even the Old Testament makes a distinction between wine and "strong drink." Entheogenic herbs are known to have frequently been added to wines in the past in order to increase their potency. In fact, according to Xenophon and Aristophanes, a wine's potency was known as its *flower*. A wine 'deficient in flower' was literally a wine to which was added an insufficient amount of flowers, leaves, and other psychoactive plant matter.[1]

> *"We hear of some so strong that they could be diluted with twenty parts water and that required at least eight party of water to be drunk safely. ... We can also document the fact that different wines were capable of inducing different physical symptoms, ranging from slumber and insomnia to hallucinations."* [2]

Thus, for Jesus' wine to have truly been superior to the wine which the guests had already enjoyed, it only stands to reason that his was something more than simple wine, and the prepared *Amanita muscaria* mushroom is perhaps the best candidate.[3]

Already having discussed the last supper and Gethesmane episodes in the previous chapter, the final indications of the *A. muscaria* mushroom that we will discuss here are the crucifixion and the sponge. From Heinrich:

> *"Every fly agaric specimen experiences death on a tree, figuratively speaking. It must go through its whole life-cycle in conjunction with its host tree and always ends up by meeting its 'death' in some form at the same tree. There must be a tree involved if it is a fly agaric. The reason for the cross...: the mushroom becomes cruciform at the end of its life. ...Jesus was given a scarlet cloak to wear over his naked body, just like the red 'cloak' of the mushroom. A 'crown of thorns' was placed on his head, which caused his head to become bloody. A look at a young fly agaric with its veil 'thorns' intact will reveal the intended meaning here. ...Being nailed to the cross...calls attention to the need for nailing both feet together on the upright, effectively giving Jesus one leg: the stipe of the mushroom."* [4]

Here, Heinrich has taken a queue from Allegro and interpreted Christ as consubstantial with the mushroom; that is, he has made them one and the same being.

The mention of the "sponge" that was used to quench Jesus' thirst during his crucifixion too may be implicative. 'Sponge' happens to be a well-known

1   Ott, Jonathan. *Pharmacotheon*, P. 156-157.
2   Wasson, R. Gordon. *The Road to Eleusis: Unveiling the Secret of the Mysteries*, P. 51-52.
3   Heinrich, Clark. *Strange Fruit: Alchemy and Religion, the Hidden Truth*, P 107.
4   *Ibid*. P. 119-120.

euphemism for mushrooms of various species. For example, in the words of Alchemist and Freemason Elias Ashmole,

> *"[The Alchemists] have said that the fruit of their tree strives up to heaven [that is, it does not hang like normal fruits], because out of the philosophic earth there arises a certain substance, like unto the branches of a loathsome sponge [or mushroom]...The point about which the whole art turns lies in the living things of nature...From a likeness not altogether remote they have called this material virgin's milk and blessed rose-colored blood...For in the blood of this stone is hidden its soul."* [5]

Other than the fly agaric mushroom, what red and white sponge grows, fruit-like, upwards from the roots of a host tree?

Once more, from Eliphas Levi:

> *"The progress of Magnetism will one day lead to the discovery of... the secret of those spongy excrescences which draw their unused surplus from trees, and surcharge themselves from their tinctures and sap; the Mushrooms, the Truffles, the Galls of trees... Then we will no more laugh at Paracelsus..."* [6]

Perhaps there is something to Allegro and Heinrich's line of argument, and more indeed lies behind the veil of the Jesus myth.

---

5   *Ibid*. P. 175.
6   Waite, Arthur Edward. *The Mysteries of Magic: A Digest of the Writings of Eliphas Levi*, P. 185.

THE PHOENIX, THE ROSE CROSS, AND THE ROYAL SECRET

There is yet another Masonic degree with undeniable Christian overtones, one that is also possessed of possible fungal undertones: the degree of *Rose+Croix* in the Southern Jurisdiction of the Ancient and Accepted Scottish Rite. Important symbols of this degree include, among others, the cross, the rose, the punishments and terrors of Hell, and the pelican.

The cross we have discussed. Regarding the rose itself, many Rosicrucian apologists such as Fludd and Maier tell us unequivocally that the rose of the Rosicrucians features the colors both red and white. The Rose+Croix being essentially a Rosicrucian degree, the same would naturally be true there. Of course, these are the same hues found tinting our fly agaric mushroom. Moreover, like a rose, the fly agaric is possessed of several tiny 'thorns'; the 'horns' of the soma 'bull' which serve to break up the soil above it.

Aside from the rose, the punishments and terrors of Hell, another feature of the degree, too are applicable. In a letter to Aldous Huxley the Canadian psychiatrist Humphry Osmond once wrote

"To fathom Hell or soar angelic, Just take a pinch of psychedelic." [1]

For, in addition to the heavenly visions of light and bliss often experienced, psychedelics also have the potential to propel one into the very depths of torturous and nightmarish Hell; enough so to make *Dante's Inferno* seem like a delightful walk in the park. Psychedelics can have the effect of facing one with his archetypal shadow, and within that face is contemplated all of the fears, guilt, and resentment at which he refuses to look during normal, waking consciousness. But, as psychoanalyst C.G. Jung theorized, confrontation with the shadow archetype is the 'apprentice-piece' on the road to

---

[1] The Telegraph. *Dr. Humphry Osmond.*

individual development.[2] And, psychedelic experience can at times be a veritable form of shadow work.

The last symbol from the Rose+Croix degree with which we're concerned is that of the pelican – perhaps the most important symbol of the set. The pelican has long been a symbol for Christ due to primitive belief that pelicans fed their young with blood by pecking at their breast. This is cleverly used in Christianity as a metaphor for Jesus' act of shedding his blood for the salvation of all mankind. However, there is no substance to this comparison. Not only do pelicans not feed their young with blood, but their beaks are fashioned in such a way so as to make pecking, especially at their own breasts, impossible. This is a mythical act, and therefore it necessitates a mythical bird. Consider the mythical phoenix bird. Similar to our Christ-like pelican, the phoenix is said to feed its chicks with blood pecked from its own breast. It also has been used by Christians to represent Jesus on account of its ability to regenerate or 'resurrect.'

> *"There are many bird analogues for the arcane substance...but none so perfectly matched to the life-cycle of the mushroom as the phoenix. It is the red firebird, hatched from an egg, which spends all of its life in its nest. It feeds its young with drops of blood, meaning that young mushrooms will be round and the colour of blood. It lifts its fiery wings and 'consumes itself' in flames, leaving nothing but 'ashes' in the nest. ...Some versions of the myth say the bird becomes a worm after it burns, an allusion to the worm infestation that is likely to occur by the time the mushroom's 'wings' are fully uplifted; when they finish their work in an unharvested specimen only worms and 'ash' remain in the nest. From its own ashes the firebird will then be reborn, whether phoenix or fly agaric."*[3]

Remarkably, the phoenix bird also appears in the degree of Master of the Royal Secret in the AASR, SJ.

At the center of the so-called *Great Masonic Camp* in the degree of Master of the Royal Secret, the phoenix, raven, and dove are depicted. The thirty-second degree, Master of the Royal Secret is the ritual wherein the *Amesha Spenta* and thus *Esfandmorz* or *Aspand*; that is, *Peganum harmala*, an ayahuasca analogue, is referenced. Therefore, special attention must here be paid. Those schooled in Alchemy will readily recognize in these birds the colors of the phases of the production of the legendary philosopher's stone; black,

---

2   Fike, Matthew A. *The One Mind: C.G. Jung and the Future of Literary Criticism*, P. 22-23.
3   Heinrich, Clark. *Strange Fruit: Alchemy and Religion, the Hidden Truth*, P. 169-170.

white, and red. Amazingly, these same birds may also be found in 16th century Alchemist Salomon Trismosin's celebrated manuscript *Splendour Solis*, where they are clearly intended to represent the three principle phases of the production of the philosopher's stone. Heinrich has identified them with the fly agaric. And, rightly so. Is it mere coincidence that these also happen to be the colors commonly associated with the phases of the development of the fly agaric mushroom? The fly agaric begins its life-cycle in the dark, black earth before emerging as a white, thorned 'egg,' covered in its universal veil. Upon maturing the veil is rent to reveal a solar redness that for all appearances burns and is reborn, not at all unlike the mythical phoenix bird.

It is possible that the *Amanita muscaria* mushroom is the mythical phoenix to which these rituals allude. As we shall see, the mushroom was not foreign to Masonic Rosicrucians and Alchemists.

MUSHROOMS AMONG ROSICRUCIANS

"He who tries to enter the Rose-garden of the Philosophers without the key is like a man wanting to walk without feet." [1]

*S*ocietas Rosicruciana In Anglia, the Mother *Society of Societas Rosicruciana In Civitatibus Foederatis*, is believed to have been formed from the ritual papers of the defunct German *Ordens Gold und Rosenkreuzer*, the first Rosicrucian Order to surface following the initial publication of the Rosicrucian manifestos in the early 17th century. Limited to Master Masons, *Ordens des Gold und Rosenkreuzer* was created by Hermann Fichtuld, a Freemason and Alchemist, and instructed its members in practical Alchemy. It is suspected that the idea for Fichtuld's Ordens des Gold und Rosenkreuzer ultimately arose from Sigmund Richter's cryptic 1710 Alchemical manuscript *The True and Perfect Preparation of the Philosopher's Stone, by the Brotherhood of the Order of the Golden and Rosy Cross*, a book which purports to name the mysterious *prima materia* or first matter of Alchemy by name, the first matter being the source from which will ultimately be prepared the *lapis philosophorum*.[2] While Richter fails to deliver on providing the name of the *prima materia*, he does offer a description of the first matter that is unmistakable for those who possess the eyes to see it.[3]

---

1   Maier, Michael. *Atalanta fugiens, emblems*, P. 31.
2   U.D., Frater. *High Magic II: Expanded Theory and Practice*, P. 272-273.
3   The only herb which Richter mentions by name is one *Helenam Vesperam*, a plant that is completely unknown to us and is mentioned without any connection to the prima materia or lapis philosophorum. *Helenam Vesperam* is recommended medicinally by Richter for the treatment of a number of symptoms, including but not limited to aches and pains, insomnia, nausea, and bronchitis. For all practical purposes, *Helenam Vesperam* could very well be an allusion to *Cannabis sativa*, the same of which is used to treat all of those symptoms. Chris Bennett, for example, in his forthcoming book *Liber 420* has identified a number of Alchemists who employed cannabis in their operations. Examples include Rebelais, Gerolamo Cardano, Robert Hooke, Avicenna, Geber, Zosimos, etc. Regarding the name of the perhaps fictional herb, Helen, daughter of Zeus, is credited in Homer's Odyssey with adding to wine a mysterious drug called *nepenthe*, which would "quiet all pain and strife and bring forgetfulness to every ill." *Vesper*, of course, means *evening star* and is an allusion to the planet Venus (Hesperus). What plant is possessed of the characteristics both of Helen's *nepenthe* and of the planet Venus or evening time?

As we've explained elsewhere, the principle goal of Alchemy is the production of the *lapis philosophorum* from the mysterious *prima materia*. The axiom states that the matter is made "not of stone, not of bone, not of metal."[4] That is to say, it comes not from the mineral kingdom and not from the animal kingdom. It must therefore be deduced that the true *prima materia* for the production of the stone of the philosophers is to be found only within the vegetable kingdom.

For a stone to meet the criteria of the true stone of the wise, it must first satisfy specific requirements, chief among them being the conferral upon its possessor of the gift of immortality. The Alchemical vocation is no vain search for physical immortality. Bodily longevity is not the variety of immortality here described. The mythologist explains rightly that

> "the search for physical immortality proceeds from a misunderstanding of the traditional teaching. On the contrary, the basic problem is: to enlarge the pupil of the eye, so that the body with its attendant personality will no longer obstruct the view. Immortality is then experienced as a present fact."[5]

Indeed, the Alchemists purport that the stone of the wise has the power to give its possessor the knowledge of his very immortal soul. Hence it also being called the *stone of projection*. For, the soul of its possessor is the very thing that appears to be projected upon the stone's proper application. Liberated from its bodily frame, the stone-projected soul is free to roam and explore the so-called astral plane, loosed from the limitations of its corporeal container – a concept that has come to be known as an *out of body experience*.

There exists a special class of truly magical and mystical plants that actually meets the above listed criteria. We speak here of *entheogens*. As the word implies, entheogenic plants are those which generate an experience of one's divinity within, that is, entheogens have the potential to facilitate what appears to be the direct experience of the reality of one's own immortal soul; of the continuity of consciousness independent of the mortal frame. The *prima materia* and *lapis philosophorum* prepared from it very likely constitute one of these plant entheogens.

In John Hamill's translation of Richter's enigmatic manuscript we read that

> "[the Prima] Materia… is found yearly which Jupiter [the Rain Bringer] fulminates with Thunder and Lightning from

---

4   Heinrich, Clark. *Magic Mushrooms in Religion and Alchemy*, P. 165.
5   Campbell, Joseph. *The Hero with a Thousand Faces*, P. 161.

> *Heaven to Earth. Our dear Brother must collect this Spirit when it is fruitful… the stems arise from one Root and from one Tree.*"[6]

Once again, there is but a single thing in nature which at once satisfies all of these requirements: an entheogenic mycorrhizal mushroom; ostensibly, the infamous red and white *Amanita muscaria*.

Like all mycorrhizal fungi, *Amanita muscaria* mushrooms can grow and subsist only within and upon the root systems of select trees (*The stems arise from one Root and from one Tree*). Richter has correctly informed his readers that the fruiting bodies of *Amanita muscaria* appear only annually, during the rainy season (*The Materia is found yearly which Jupiter [the Rain Bringer] fulminates… Our dear Brother must collect this Spirit when it is fruitful…*). And, it was believed that flashes of lightning increased their number (*…fulminates with Thunder and Lightning*), a bit of mycological folklore that in 2010 was actually proven to be scientific fact.[7] Yes indeed, the *Amanita muscaria* mushroom would appear to solve the problem of Richter's curious *prima materia*.

To our knowledge, the first author to propose that the secret of the Alchemists' *materia* and *lapis* may be the *Amanita muscaria* mushroom was researcher Clark Heinrich in his 1995 book *Strange Fruit*. And, as Heinrich ably demonstrates, Richter was not the first Alchemist to likely allude to the *Amanita muscaria* mushroom as being the *materia*, source of the *lapis* in Alchemy.[8] Here follows a few descriptions from various Alchemical (and one Kabbalistic) manuscripts, all of which seem to point to the *Amanita muscaria* mushroom.

> "*Likewise [the Alchemists] have said that the fruit of their tree strives up to heaven [as opposed to down toward the earth], because out of the philosophic earth there arises a certain substance, like unto the branches of a loathsome sponge… The point about which the whole [Alchemical] art turns lies in the living things of nature… From a likeness not altogether remote they have called this material virgin's milk and blessed rose-colored blood… For in the blood of this stone is hidden its soul.*" – *Theatricum Chemicum Brittanicum*[9]

---

6   Gilbert, R.A. *The True and Perfect Preparation of the Philosopher's Stone, by the Brotherhood of the Order of the Golden and Rosy Cross*, P. 5, 14.
7   Ryall, Julian. *Lightning Makes Mushrooms Multiply*.
8   The *prima materia* here alludes to the mushroom itself, and the *lapis philosophorum*, to the compound, in stone or elixir form, prepared from the fungus.
9   Heinrich, Clark. *Strange Fruit: Alchemy and Religion, the Hidden Truth*. P. 175.

"His soul rises up from [the secret substance] and is exalted to the heavens, that is, to the spirit, and becomes the red rising sun, waxing in Luna into the nature of the sun. And then the lantern with two lights [red and white], which is the water of life, will return to its origin, that is, to earth. And it becomes of low estate, is humbled and decays, and is joined to its beloved, the terrestrial sulphur." – Consilium Coniugii[10]

"The secret of secrets: Out of the scorching noon of Isaac, out of the dregs of wine, a fungus emerged, a cluster, male and female together, red as a rose, expanding in many directions and paths. The [red] male is called Sama'el, his [white] female is always included within him. Just as it is on the side of holiness, so it is on the other side: male and female embracing one another." – Zohar Sitrei Torah 1:47b - 148b[11]

"White-skinned lady, lovingly joined to her red-limbed husband, wrapped in each other's arms in the bliss of connubial union, merge and dissolve as they come to the goal of [the perfected stone]..." – Rosarium Philosophorum[12]

"[The stone's] father is the [red] sun, its mother the [white] moon; the wind has carried it in its belly; its nurse is the earth. Its power is complete when it is turned toward the earth. It ascends from earth to heaven, and descends again to earth, and receives the power of the higher and lower things. So will you have the glory of the whole world." – Tabula Smaragdina[13]

Regarding this last quotation, Heinrich elaborates:

"Read as [an Amanita muscaria] metaphor the Tabula quotation reveals a hidden meaning: the secret substance's father is the sunlike mature mushroom, whose 'seed' falls from his body to bring about the birth of his offspring. Its mother is the white, rough-textured 'moon' of the [egg-shaped] mushroom embryo, which seems to give birth to the solar cap. The wind carries the mushroom spores

---

10   Ibid. P. 169.
11   Matt, Daniel Chanan. *Zohar, the Book of Enlightenment*, P. 77.
12   Heinrich, Clark. *Strange Fruit: Alchemy and Religion, the Hidden Truth*, P. 167
13   Ibid. P. 165.

> *as well as the storms that bring about the birth. The earth 'nurses' the mushroom from egg to cup as the mushroom draws water from it. 'When it turns toward the earth' corresponds to the end of sporulation, when the upturned cap begins to dry out and turn back toward the ground; this is the optimal harvest time, because fully mature mushrooms have the highest concentrations of muscimol, the main active ingredient. Drying converts [the toxic] ibotenic acid to [the entheogenic] muscimol as well; once completely dry 'its power is complete,' but not before."* [14]

Heinrich shows that Amanita muscaria mushrooms contain a potent poison called ibotenic acid. As the fruiting body matures, much of this acid is converted into the desired muscimol, the entheogenic agent of the fungus, and even more is converted upon drying. Therefore, fully matured specimens are prized over 'green' ones.[15]

Even in the rituals we find potential allusions to the *Amanita muscaria* mushroom. Consider, for example, the following excerpt from the *Practicus* lecture, *Practicus* being the Grade wherein we as Rosicrucians are invited to investigate the Alchemical art.

> *"Many indeed were the processes devised, but there was a general consensus of opinion that the last three stages of the [Al]chemical process were marked by a series of colour changes, from Black through White to Red; this red matter was the Philosopher's Stone, or Red Elixir, which could transmute Silver into Gold."* [16]

In all probability, the "red [first?] matter" refers to the bright red pileus or cap of the mushroom, from which the *Red Elixir* or *Philosopher's Stone* is prepared. It proceeds from the *black* earth as a small, *white*, egg-shaped mass. From this mass emerges the brilliant *red* fruiting body or mushroom proper. The color scheme may also relate to the mature mushroom specimen itself. Truly, one Alchemist and Rosicrucian apologist praised the Hermetic matter as follows:

> *"Thy face is red [and] thy bosom is whiter than purest snow. Thy feet are shod with black sandals..."* [17]

---

14 Ibid.
15 "The Alchemists wrote that the Green Lion denotes ripeness, not color." – Clark Heinrich, privately communicated
16 S.R.I.C.F. *First Order Ritual*, P. 58.
17 Maier, Michael. *A Subtle Allegory: Concerning the Secrets of Alchemy.*

Such is an adequate description of a harvested specimen, with its brilliant red pileus facing the sun, its pure white lamellae and stipe below, and its bulbous volva at the base covered in the moist black remnants of the dank earth.

The transmutation of base metals into gold is another common Alchemical metaphor that refers to the illumination or enlightenment (hence *gold*) of the uninitiated man (i.e., base metal) that results from the proper application of the *lapis philosophorum*.

The *Practicus* lecture continues:

> "*The Alchymysts… endeavoured to produce from certain herbs an Elixir Vitae, which should have power to prolong life and restore health to the sick.*" [18]

This latter supposition stems naturally from the fallacious notion that the Alchemists' *lapis* literally conferred upon its possessor the gift of physical immortality. But, as was explained above in the third paragraph, the misguided quest for bodily longevity proceeds from a blatant misunderstanding of the traditional teaching. Even so, it should be noted that in the *Practicus* lecture the *Elixir Vitae* is specifically purported to be prepared not from minerals, stones, or metals, but from "certain herbs."

Other Alchemical systems describe the color process as moving from black to red, and thence to white, as is reflected in the lecture for the *Rose+Croix* degree in the Ancient and Accepted Scottish Rite, Southern Jurisdiction. However, *Societas Rosicruciana In Civitatibus Foederatis* has opted to instruct Her *Fratres* in an alternate scheme. There is only one naturalistic explanation of which we can conceive for why that would be the case.

We close this investigation into the mycological nature of Richter's *prima materia* with a poem by Clark Heinrich titled *Our Water*.

> *An aching heart*
> *A king starts to waken*
> *Harken back to olden days*
> *An alchemist beckons again*
> *What's old is new, he says*
> *And everything is shaken*
> *Retort, vial and vas are broken*
> *Even earth is quaking*
> *A shaking hand betakes the potion*
> *– this is not the time to weaken –*
> *Puts the chalice to his lips*

---

[18] S.R.I.C.F. *First Order Ritual*, P. 58.

And pours the liquor down
He cries 'Elixir!
Rosy blood of God!
Living waters truly!
Holy tincture of my Art
Lift me up to heaven's door –
Cleanse my mind and heal my heart!'
Then having drunk he drinks once more[19]

---

19   Heinrich, Clark. *Strange Fruit: Alchemy and Religion, the Hidden Truth*, P. 160.

ALEISTER AND AMANITAS

Beginning his fraternal career in the SRIA-inspired Hermetic Order of the Golden Dawn, the English occultist Aleister Crowley was Raised to the Sublime Degree of Master Mason in Anglo-Saxon Lodge No. 343 under the *Grande Loge de France* on Dec. 17, 1904. Four years prior, he had been made a 33° in an irregular form of Scottish Rite Freemasonry in Mexico by a man named Don Jesus Medina, whose system may have been a form of Cerneauism.[1] Crowley would later go on to become the O.H.O. of the fringe Masonic order *Ordo Templi Orientis*, which he eventually reworked to reflect his magico-religious system *Thelema*. He also founded a magical Order called *Fraternitatis A∴A∴* that drew heavily upon the Hermetic Order of the Golden Dawn but differs primarily in that, like the O.T.O. after Crowley, the A∴A∴ is inherently Thelemic.

Crowley was notorious for his penned practical pranks, from discussing sex magick in terms of diabolical child sacrifice to potentially discussing psychedelic drug use under the cloak of sex magick. Crowley was a master of the art of *obscurum per obscurius*; of 'explaining the obscure by means of the more obscure.' While we know from his diaries that he certainly was wont to engage in magick of the sexual variety, it is our suspicion that, in at least some instances, when Crowley was outwardly explaining sex magick in his books, he may well have actually been discussing the occult use of *Amanita muscaria* mushrooms, which, would be in perfect keeping with his *modus operandi*.

Sex magick is a sort of Western Tantra whereby practitioners believe they enter into heightened states of consciousness or acquire powers via various sexual acts, including but not limited to the ritual consumption of semen and menstrual blood. This latter method takes center stage in *Liber XV*, better known as the *Gnostic Mass*, the "only truly Official Ritual" of *Ecclesiae Gnosticae Catholicae*, the ecclesiastical branch of *Crowley's Ordo Templi Orientis*. (Sabazius) Crowley was not the first self-proclaimed Gnostic to engage in said behavior. Saint Augustine accused even Mani and the Manicheans of consuming communion wafers that were covered in menses and splattered with semen.

---

1   Starr, Martin P. *Aleister Crowley: Freemason!*

However, this imagery is not unique to the various Gnostic sects. Indeed, according to a private communication from Kagyu lay lama Mike Crowley, the Tantric system known as Vajrayana Buddhism has been employing this symbolism for centuries, in order to secretly indicate to initiates the *A. muscaria* mushroom, also known as the *fly agaric*. The menses allegedly alludes to the brilliant red pileus, the splattered semen to the white remnants of the universal veil that mottle the top. And, as Ruck, Hoffman, and Celdran point out in their book *Mushrooms, Myth, and Mithras*, Mani and the Manicheans were also accused of venerating a certain "red mushroom."[2]

In addition to sex, Crowley was known to incorporate a number of methods into his magick, chief among them being the use of drugs. For example, *Liber CMXXXIV vel The Cactus* records a number of magical experiments conducted by Crowley using the mescaline-rich *Anhalonium lewenii* (reclassified as *Lophophora williamsii*) cactus, aka peyote. However, aside from depicting a specimen in his painting *May Morn* that was published in *Equinox Vol. III No. 1*, we have been unable to locate any reference he himself directly made to the *A. muscaria* mushroom. This is itself an oddity. For, like Lewis Carroll before him, Crowley would have no doubt been familiar with Mordecai Cooke's 1860 book *The Seven Sisters of Sleep*. Cooke's book details the seven most popular narcotic plants of the Victorian era. As one would expect from a perfectionist such as Crowley, all of the drugs named by Cooke have been carefully allotted to the *Vegetable Drugs* column of Crowley's *Liber 777* – all save one: the *Amanita muscaria* mushroom.[3] Another oddity is the curious attribution of Elixir Vitae to path one in the *Vegetable Drugs* column. [4]Most of Crowley's acolytes are prone to interpret *Elixir Vitae* as being a veiled allusion to sexual fluids. But sexual fluids are anything but vegetable in nature. For all of its tidiness, the careless attribution of sexual fluids to a column titled *Vegetable Drugs* would seem to this author wholly inconsistent for a text as symmetrical and rounded as is *Liber 777*.

It is also likely that Crowley encountered a reference to *A. muscaria* mushrooms in the writings of Sir Richard Frances Burton, who was named by Crowley an official saint of the *Ecclesiae Gnosticae Catholicae*. In a footnote to his 1862 work *The Look of the West 1860: Across the Plains to California*, Burton states that "there is actually [a] kind of cactus called by the whites 'whiskey-root,' and by the Indian 'peioke' [i.e. *peyote*] used like the

---

2   Ruck, Carl A.P. *Mushrooms, Myth and Mithras: The Drug Cult that Civilized Europe.*, P. 24, 173.
3   Granted there is no mention by name of betel nut in Liber 777. However, betel nut may well have been lumped into the "All cerebral excitants" entry allotted to path twelve. Compared to the more powerful cocaine to which he was accustomed, betel nut may have appeared to Crowley as more or less of an afterthought.
4   Regardie, Israel. *777 and Other Qabalistic Writings of Aleister Crowley*, P. 212.

intoxicating mushroom of Siberia [i.e. *A. muscaria*]."[5] Furthermore, Paracelsus, another Crowley-named saint of the *Ecclesiae Gnosticae Catholicae*, too makes reference to an "agaric" mushroom which, in response to line from Rebelias, he contrasts with a certain "manna."[6] For, at least twice Rebelias potentially alludes to the fly agaric mushroom as "the good agaric."[7] Note that Rabelais is thought to be the ultimate source for Aleister Crowley's *Law of Thelema*: "Do what thou wilt."[8] It is therefore exceedingly unlikely that the mushroom could have escaped Crowley's attention. Also of interest is the account of Anthony Stansfeld Jones, the adopted son of Charles Stansfeld Jones, aka Frater Achad, the "magical son" of Aleister Crowley, regarding Frater Achad's obsessive preoccupation with a "poisonous" mushroom, which he spent untold hours searching for in the wooded area behind his home.[9] Was Achad in search of *A. muscaria*?

In 1995, in his book *Strange Fruit*, Clark Heinrich speculated that the famed *Elixir Vitae* of the Alchemists was the *Soma*-like psychoactive juice pressed from mature, dried and reconstituted *A. muscaria* mushroom caps.[10] If Heinrich is correct, then it stands to reason that knowledge of the entheogenic properties of *A. muscaria* mushrooms could have survived well into Crowley's day. Might he have been aware of them? Is the *Elixir Vitae* entry in *Liber 777* an allusion to *A. muscaria*? Were any other of Crowley's references to sexual fluids fungal suggestions? It is at present nearly impossible to say. But, until we read in Mike Crowley's work that references to semen and menstrual blood are commonly employed in Tantric Buddhist empowerments as allusions to the *A. muscaria* mushroom, we had never questioned Aleister Crowley's use of that same imagery within the context of his own Western Tantra.

Why Crowley should keep secret a powerful and well-known psychoactive drug, especially after speaking so open and plainly about so many others, e.g., hashish, peyote, belladonna, cocaine, opium, etc. etc., is the next question. Perhaps it was due to an oath of secrecy. The only safe thing we can say at this point is that obligations of secrecy never stopped Aleister Crowley from writing before.

---

5   Burton, Sir Richard Francis. *The City of the Saints: And Across the Rocky Mountains to California*, P. 64.
6   Weeks, Andrew. *Paracelsus*, P. 32.
7   Plattard, Jean. *The Life of Francois Rabelais*, P. 204.
8   *Liber AL vel Legis*, 3:60
9   Stanfeld-Jones, Tony. *Thelema Coast to Coast*, Episode No. 4.
10   Heinrich, Clark. *Strange Fruit: Alchemy and Religion, the Hidden Truth*, P. 8-12.

PYTHAGORAS' HECATOMB

So, has symbolism pointing to *Amanita muscaria* mushrooms been preserved in the three degrees of Craft Freemasonry? It is certainly possible. To begin with, there is a potential indicator in the Master Mason degree. Albert Pike, in his *Morals and Dogma*, translated the substitute word of a Master Mason as "Son of putrefaction."[1] Insofar as fruiting bodies are oftentimes birthed from the decomposition of their host, the mushroom would most certainly answer to the epithet of *Son of putrefaction*.

Another possible indication of mushroom symbolism in the Craft degrees is found in the spurious account of Pythagoras' curious hecatomb episode, wherein he is said to have sacrificed one hundred oxen. Considering the fact that Pythagoras not only eschewed and condemned the sacrifice of animals of any kind, for ritual purposes or otherwise, and that he was a devout vegetarian, interpreted in anything other than a cryptic and symbolic light, his actions appear both barbaric and bizarre. Whatever type of bulls Pythagoras allegedly slaughtered, they were not of flesh and blood. Of course, neither was the *Soma Bull*.

Masonic ritual informs us that, upon discovering his famous theorem, Pythagoras exclaimed "Eureka!" and subsequently sacrificed a hecatomb. Insofar as it was Archimedes and not Pythagoras who cried "Eureka!" upon making his important discovery, and provided that Pythagoras was a vegetarian who condemned animal sacrifice, the contemplative Mason is immediately struck with the notion that something is not quite right with said portion of the ritual. In our experience, blatant inconsistencies within Masonic ritual are quite literally invitations to the contemplative Mason to investigate the matters further and, meditating upon this particular matter, we have approached two interesting points. Firstly, Pythagoras allegedly made his exclamation after discovering a means to try a right angle or square. Archimedes, on the other hand, cried "Eureka!" after discovering a way to try gold; displacement. Secondly, the vegetarian Pythagoras purportedly followed up his discovery with the absurd act of sacrificing a hecatomb. Similarly, the reasonable and scientific Archimedes,

---

1   De Hoyos, Arturo. *Albert Pike's Morals and Dogma: Annotated Edition*, P. 746.

following his discovery, absurdly leaped from his bathtub and ran throughout the streets of the town nude. In both cases, there is a remarkable scientific discovery followed by an equally remarkable act of absurdity.

Consider the Old Testament analogue of Moses' destruction of the golden calf. Like Pythagoras, Moses destroyed a bovine symbol. And, like Archimedes, Moses put the gold into water. Furthermore, Moses' acts were committed following his discovery of a means to try the Jewish people: the ten commandments. After this, the prophet too did something quite absurd. From Heinrich,

> *"After his first forty days on the mountain Moses returned with the Tablets of the Pretext and was shocked to see the people dancing and fornicating in front of a gold bull. The worship of God as a bull was happening at the time in several places, including Canaan, Syria, and of course India, where the 'bull' was the red mushroom that turns to gold when it dries. Which form of bull worship the Israelites were performing is not known, but once again there are curious similarities to the ritual use of fly agaric in other areas. We are told that Moses 'burned' the bull and ground it to powder, which, unless the bull had been made of wood and merely coated with gold, would not have been possible. He then put the powder in water and made all the participants drink. This sounds more like a ritual than a form of punishment, but punishment comes swift and sure after the drinking episode. 'Put the bull-plant next to fire until it becomes golden and so dry that it is easily powdered. Mix the powder with water and drink.' These imagined instructions give a sophisticated recipe not only for bringing about the vital chemical changes that drying produces, but also for getting the mushroom into the stomach without chewing it [chewing A. muscaria can cause nausea or vomiting]. Whatever the Israelites were really doing in Moses' absence is unknown, but the inclusion of the bull-burning episode in the story seems to be another misplaced remnant of cultic mushroom practice."* [2]

Likewise, whatever Pythagoras was really doing is unknown, but the inclusion of the hecatomb episode in Masonic ritual, paired with the apparently intentional mix-up of Pythagoras with Archimedes, also seems to be another "remnant of cultic mushroom practice." In combining the Pythagoras and Archimedes stories in this way it is our suspicion that, similar to Moses' Biblical golden calf episode, in all probability the fly agaric mushroom is directly implied. Moreover, we have already seen that in its various phases,

---

2   Heinrich, Clark. *Strange Fruit: Alchemy and Religion, the Hidden Truth*, P. 82.

the fly agaric mushrooms have been likened to both bulls and to animal hides. Eureka!

THE HOOPOE-BIRD AND THE SHAMIR WORM

Next, consider the *shamir* worm of Jewish lore. In the Entered Apprentice degree the candidate learns that "at the building of King Solomon's Temple, there was not heard the sound of an axe, hammer, or any tool of iron." The explanation provided for this oddity is that

> "the stones were hewed, squared, and numbered at the quarries where they were raised; the trees felled and prepared in the forests of Lebanon, carried by sea in floats to Joppa, and from thence by land to Jerusalem, where they were set up with wooden mauls, prepared for that purpose."

It is our opinion that the explanation provided by the Fraternity is far less interesting than that offered by the Jewish religion from which the legend was derived. As in Masonic tradition, no tool of iron was said to have been heard in the Jewish legend, but it isn't because the ashlars were prepared at the quarry. Rather, no tool, iron or otherwise, was said to have been employed at all. According to legend, the stones of the Temple were instead cut with the aid of a magical, living object called the *shamir*.

Using a single "grain" of shamir that was no larger than a "barley-corn," Solomon was able to fashion all of the stones for the building of the Temple. Similarly, Moses before him had used the shamir to carve the mysterious *urim* and *thummim*, the 'visionary' breast plate and its embellished stones worn by the high priest.

Described variously as a green stone and a living worm, the shamir would cut through even the hardest of substances simply by having them "shown" to it. For this reason the shamir had to be kept in a box of fleece, the only material that could withstand its gaze. As we have already seen, fleece has its own agaric connotations.

The legend relates that after creating the shamir on the sixth day of creation,

> *"God gave the shamir to the hoopoe-bird…for safekeeping. The hoopoe promised to guard it with her life; for eons, she kept it with her at all times, safe in the Garden of Eden. Sometimes, when the hoopoe flew throughout the earth, she kept the little worm tight in her beak, departing with it only to cleft open rocks on desolate mountains, that she might seed them and cause vegetation to blossom forth and provide her with food. …Where did the hoopoe keep such a powerful creature? What ordinary vessel could possibly hold it? Since lead alone could resist the hoopoe's bite, the bird sealed up her precious charge inside a box of lead, wrapped in a woolen cloth nestled among a handful of barley grains. And there she might have kept it forever had not Solomon needed it to build the Holy Temple in Jerusalem."* [1]

Another version relates that the "Prince of the Sea" had given the shamir worm to a remote mountain "woodcock" for safe keeping. Solomon sent his men to find the bird's nest and retrieve the mysterious shamir. When they discovered the nest empty the men placed over it a sheet of glass. Upon returning and finding his nest so covered, the mountain bird used the shamir to break the glass and uncover his nest. When the bird was settled the men intentionally frightened him away, thereby causing him to drop the shamir worm, leaving it behind. At that point the shamir was retrieved from the nest and delivered to Solomon.

The hoopoe-bird and shamir worm are clearly linked, just like the phoenix bird and the worm which is found in its nest following the former's spontaneous combustion. It is our suspicion that we have here a possible reference to the phoenix, and therefore another potential allusion to the *Amanita muscaria* mushroom. Moreover, we are told in the Jewish legend, that this bird was somehow responsible for perfecting the ashlars used in building Solomon's Temple. As every member of the Craft knows, the rough ashlar represents the unperfected Mason. The perfect ashlar, on the other hand, represents the perfected Mason. Thus, it is not difficult to see how this particular bird (and worm) might be said to have perfected the ashlars for use in Solomon's temple; that is, how the *Amanita muscaria* mushroom might be a veritable tool for initiation and transcendence. Recall what Heinrich had to say about the fungal, feathered phoenix:

---

1   J.H.O.M. *A Magical Worm Called Shamir.*

"There are many bird analogues for the arcane substance...but none so perfectly matched to the life-cycle of the mushroom as the phoenix. ...Some versions of the myth say the bird becomes a worm after it burns, an allusion to the worm infestation that is likely to occur by the time the mushroom's 'wings' are fully uplifted; when they finish their work in an unharvested specimen only worms and 'ash' remain in the nest..." [2]

---

2   Heinrich, Clark. *Strange Fruit: Alchemy and Religion, the Hidden Truth*, P. 169-170.

CONCLUDING REMARKS

> *"The seat of divine inspiration lies beyond the veil. He who would receive the gift of Wisdom must be prepared to surrender to it completely, as it may spring forth suddenly, without warning, and from the darkness. Once received, it cannot be undone. Woe unto him who partakes of the mysteries unworthily, for he may lose himself where the true initiate finds reality unveiled."* [1]

These words have been borrowed from the synopsis of the Knight of the Sun or Prince Adept degree as the same has been given in the *Scottish Rite Ritual Monitor and Guide*. But, they are perfectly applicable to the entheogenic explorer as well. Like so many fruiting bodies, the revelations of one bemushroomed spring forth suddenly, without warning, and from the darkness. And, once the veil of reality has been rent, he must surrender to the rapture completely lest he find himself lost amidst a sea of changing visions, boundless, more than a little frightened and confused. When the veil is torn then with one's perception is expanded his very consciousness. By degrees he becomes enlightened. To quote William Blake,

> *"If the doors of perception were cleansed everything would appear to man as it is, infinite."* [2]

As the late visionary comedian Bill Hicks once mused, "entheogens are like Windex® for those perceptual doors."[3]

One may well argue that the visions resulting from the ingestion of entheogenic plants are mere illusions; little more than apparitions or hallucinations. However, as researchers at Johns Hopkins have pointed out, entheogen-induced visions meet all of the psychiatric criteria for "complete mystical experience." Visions induced by entheogens and spontaneous spiritual experience are so similar in fact that there currently exists no set standard to distinguish one

---

1 De Hoyos, Arturo. *Scottish Rite Ritual Monitor and Guide*, P. 645.
2 Blake, William. *The Marriage of Heaven and Hell*, P. xii.
3 TV Tropes. *Bill Hicks*

from the other. They appear to be two types of the same phenomenon.[4] Moreover, entheogenic transcendence may well be directly implied within Masonic ritual itself where, in the Fellowcraft degree, long before the death experienced by the Master Mason is suffered, the candidate for Fellowship is taken up in a whirling ascent to the symbolic middle chamber, wherein, in addition to reaping his karma-like wages, he is granted a vision of the emblematic representative of deity Himself – along with a prevalent "Geometry." This portion of Masonic ritual is the very stuff of entheogenic experience. Correspondingly, in the Emulation ritual of Freemasonry, the Fellowcraft is rightfully permitted to extend his "researches into the hidden mysteries of nature." The psychoactive properties of entheogenic plants, as well as the visions resulting from their ingestion, would certainly constitute the *hidden mysteries of nature*.

As was said in the opening prayer,

> *"Give us grace diligently to search thy word in the book of nature, wherein the duties of our high vocation are inculcated with Divine authority."*

All religions and spiritual disciplines are manmade. All holy books, claims to divine inspiration notwithstanding, were written by men. As one Mahatma articulated it, "God has no religion." Nature is arguably the only thing that was actually created by deity. Since plant entheogens occur naturally, they are a divinely intended means by which man can glimpse the divine. This is not to say that religious dedication or adhering to spiritual disciplines is fruitless. There are a number of endogenous psychoactive compounds, including DMT and endocannabinoids, as well as the more familiar serotonin and dopamine, that can be triggered through prayer, music, meditation, fasting, yoga, exercise, sleep or sensory deprivation, etc. However, it is our suspicion that many of these mechanisms were likely triggered accidentally or were later technical developments through concentrated effort, and long before the invention of conventional religion and spiritual disciplines man was transcending mundane reality and communing with the 'Other' via the ingestion of naturally occurring plant sacraments found in his environment. Entheogens, we will venture, may be the *lost word*, and religion, the *substitute*.

However, this is not to say that entheogens are the only valid path to attainment. Nor is it to say that their use should be continued at all times along that path. In part, Mastership is about acquiring balance. If we develop to any degree in one direction, we must necessarily extend our efforts toward the opposite. If one attains a state via the use of entheogenic plants, it is important that he also seek to acquire that same experience through his own efforts. This

---

4   Hughes, Michael M. *Sacred Intentions: Inside the Johns Hopkins Psilocybin Studies.*

is not to say that the goal of the work is to eventually trip out or hallucinate perpetually without the use of drugs. That would be useless, for both us and for society. The aim here can be formulated thusly: If one can ingest, say, 125mg of pure MDMA and suddenly and completely, wholeheartedly, forgive his enemies, then at the very least it should demonstrate to him that his *self* is not quite as fixed as his ego would have him perceive. On the contrary, we are fluid; mercurial; reflective. Being so, we can change for the better. Through personal effort and over time, like the Alchemist's art upon his first matter, we can perfect ourselves. If a drug can do this, we can do this. Moreover, what use is the revelation that we are in a sense all one if we do not allow that vision to inform our daily behavior after we have reintegrated into waking consciousness? We fail to see it.

We hereby close this study into the presence of entheogenic symbolism within Masonic ritual.

CONCLUDING REMARKS

PART IV:
SUPPLEMENTAL PAPERS ON PSILOCYBIN MUSHROOMS

PSILOCYBE CUBENSIS: A WORTHY CANDIDATE FOR THE PHILOSOPHER'S STONE

> *"Who is wise, and understandeth this, of which Alphidius saith, that men and children pass her by daily in the streets and public places, and she is trodden into the mire by beasts of burden and by cattle?"*
> – *Pseudo-Aquinas*[1]

While the diaphanous veil which once obscured the searching gaze of the profane from Alchemy's innermost secrets certainly remains intact, it has nevertheless begun to fray and unravel at the seams, exposing portions of her many mysteries to those patient students who still retain sight enough to see her for the desirable maiden that the entire civilized world once knew her to be. The principle goal of the Alchemists was (and is) the production of the lapis philosophorum; the philosopher's stone or stone of the wise. We now know that there are not one but many stones. For, in true Alchemy the term stone refers merely to the crystalline salts (a veritable stone) which may be extracted or produced, to use Alchemical terminology, from certain plant sources. And, in some instances (as in the case of the present study), the stone refers to the very plant itself. As the Alchemical axiom states, the lapis philosophorum is "not of stone, not of bone, not of metal."[2] That is to say, it comes not from the mineral kingdom and not from the animal kingdom. It must therefore be deduced that the true stone of the philosophers is to be found only within the plant kingdom. Unfortunately, many Alchemists are content to produce stones from virtually any mineral, metal, plant, or animal, ascribing the value of those stones solely to their possessed planetary signatures. However, for a stone to meet the criteria of the true stone of the wise, an imagined planetary signature will not suffice. It must first satisfy specific requirements, chief among these being the conferral upon its possessor of the gift of immortality.

1   Jung, C.G. *The Collected Works*, P. 5903.
2   Heinrich, Clark. *Strange Fruit: Alchemy and Religion, the Hidden Truth*, P. 165.

Let it be said that the Alchemical vocation is no vain search for physical immortality. Bodily longevity is not the variety of immortality here described. The mythologist explains rightly that

> *"[the] search for physical immortality proceeds from a misunderstanding of the traditional teaching. On the contrary, the basic problem is: to enlarge the pupil of the eye, so that the body with its attendant personality will no longer obstruct the view. Immortality is then experienced as a present fact..."* [3]

Indeed! The Alchemists purport that the stone of the wise has the power to give its possessor the knowledge of his very immortal soul. Hence it also being called the stone of projection. For, the soul of its possessor is the very thing that is projected upon the stone's proper application. Liberated from its bodily frame, the stone-projected soul is free to roam and explore the so-called astral plane. Similar to the Vedic soma, the possessor of the lapis philosophorum

> *"finds himself both linked to his external body, and yet away from it in his spiritual form. The latter, freed from the former, soars for the time being in the ethereal higher regions, becoming virtually 'as one of the gods,' and yet preserving in his physical brain the memory of what he sees and learns."* [4]

As for the initiates of the Greater Mystery celebrated at Eleusis, the Alchemists purport that the possessor of the true stone has the ability to leave "[his] own identity [and] become at home with the gods."[5]

Conveniently, there exists in nature a special class of truly magical and mystical plants that actually satisfies the above listed criteria. We speak here of entheogens. As the word implies, entheogenic plants are those which generate an experience of one's divinity within; that is, entheogens have the potential to facilitate the direct experience of the reality of one's own immortal soul; of the continuity of individual consciousness independent of the mortal frame. Such being the case, there is one entheogenic plant that is of particular interest to us for our present purpose. For, said plant is truly the coveted key which helps decipher a number of obscure and esoteric Alchemical references and riddles.

A note discovered in the back flyleaf of a copy of E.A. Hitchcock's classic study *Remarks Upon Alchemy* (1857) and communicated to us privately by Clark Heinrich reads:

[3]   Campbell, Joseph. *The Hero with a Thousand Faces*, P. 161.
[4]   Blavatsky, H.P. *The Secret Doctrine: The Synthesis of Science, Religion, and Philosophy*, P. 499.
[5]   Eyer, Shawn. *Psychedelic Effects and the Eleusinian Mysteries*.

> "the Secret of our Stone…shall shew itself forth as though it bloomed sweetly upon the dunghill. And if you shall ask me what it resembles – I shall say to you that it lives and is to be found in the likeness and form of many things in Nature. For it can be as the Moon as has been said – If they say the Moon is blue, we must believe that it is true. – But this only if molested, for the colour of the Moon is white in its naturalistic State."

What other than the *Psilocybe cubensis* mushroom meets the criteria of being at once a living thing in nature that, in addition to 'blooming' upon dung, also appears as the moon, i.e. round and pale, unless the same has been "molested," in which case it then turns blue?

Psilocybe cubensis is a coprophilic mushroom meaning that it can only subsist upon the dung of certain species. Its psychoactive constituents are a pair of powerful compounds termed psilocin and psilocybin, first synthesized by Swiss chemist Albert Hoffman and brought to the attention of the Western world by amateur mycologist R. Gordon Wasson. Although pale in its undisturbed state, the *Psilocybe cubensis* mushroom has the unique characteristic of staining blue when bruised or broken. This reaction is due to the oxidation of the psilocin and psilocybin contained in the mushroom, and serves as an easy identifier for inclined fungus foragers.

Alchemist and Rosicrucian apologist Count Michael Maier provides us with yet another allusion to the stone as *P. cubensis*.

> "But every man ought to take care that he be very well acquainted with those Dragons that are to be joined to the Charriot of Triptolemus before he undertake any thing, for they are Winged and Volatile, and if you desire to know them you will find them in the Philosophickal Dung. For they are Dung and generated from Dung, and are that Vessel which Maria affirms not to be Necromantick but that Regiment of your Fire without which you will effect nothing. I have disclosed the Truth to You which I have gathered out of the monuments of the Ancients by incredible labour and the expense of many years."[6]

Here Maier informs us emphatically that these "Dragons," without which the Alchemist is sadly impotent, are to be found only upon dung, wherefrom they are generated. They are "Winged and Volatile" insofar as they, when unfixed from their dung heap, possess the potential to project the soul of the

---

6   Maier, Michael. "The Alchemy Website." *Atalanta fugiens, emblems*

Alchemist into astral flight. Again, without these "Dragons," the Alchemist can accomplish nothing. It is as Morienus has warned: the Alchemist must

> *"[take] that which is trodden underfoot upon the dunghill; if [he does] not, when [he wishes] to climb the stairs, [he] will fall down upon [his] head."* [7]

The reference to Triptolemus also is significant. Triptolemus symbolically presided over the threshing floor at the Greater Mystery celebrated at Eleusis, where the entheogenic fungus ergot was ceremonially separated from its host (rye) for the same to be used in the sacred initiatory beverage kykeon.[8] Furthermore, Triptolemus' "Chariot" may loosely be likened to the *merkabah* or throne-chariot of Ezekiel's vision, which is believed by Kabbalists to be the mechanism that propels practitioners into the lofty, celestial regions upon mystical ascension. It is further notable that the visionary prophet Ezekiel is said in verse fifteen of chapter four of his book to have curiously made his bread from cow's dung.

Moving on to other dung references in Alchemy, in A.E. Waite's *The Hermetic and Alchemical Writings of Paracelsus* we find:

> *"The natural mumia should be compounded out of three chief antimonies so that the foreign microcosm should govern the physical body, whether by means of the element water or by means of its metals, salts, etc., or otherwise by means of the element of earth, as by its herbs and boleti, or in tereniabin or nostoch. For all these are mansions of the supercelestial things."* [9]

In response to this cryptic jargon Waite adds:

> *"Boleti. Boletus is a mushroom. Bolitus is the same as Bolbiton, i.e., the excrement of oxen. These explanations will, perhaps, not throw much light on the use of the term by Paracelsus."* [10]

Why would Waite wish to draw connections between a mushroom and the excrement of oxen in regard to Paracelsus? Does he mean to insinuate that, like Britten and Levi, Paracelsus perhaps knew something of entheogenic coprophilic fungi?

7   Jung, C.G. *The Collected Works*, P. 5955.
8   Ruck, Carl A.P. *Sacred Mushrooms of the Goddess and the Secrets of Eleusis*, P. 121-145.
9   De Laurence, L.W. *The Hermetic and Alchemical Writings of Aureolus Phillippus Theophrastus Bombast of Hohenheim, Called Paracelsus, the Great by A.E. Waite*, P. 342.
10   *Ibid.*, P. 357.

The final Alchemical allusion to the *Psilocybe cubensis* mushroom as the lapis philosophorum which will be discussed here comes from Andreas Libavius' 1606 manuscript *Alchymia*, allegedly the most widely read of the Alchemical books of the era.[11] Preserved in this text are a number of fascinating drawings of Alchemical apparatus. Included among these is an oddity labeled a "Dung bath" (with corresponding "Muffle for dung bath") that is no doubt an early terrarium of some sort, possibly designed from the production of *P. cubensis* mushrooms within the comfort of the Alchemists laboratory. Furthermore, when placed atop its base and turned a mere ninety degrees, this "Muffle" and "Dung bath" resemble nothing so much as the cap and stipe of a fruiting body. The implication would appear to be a mushroom of the coprophilic variety such as our stone *Psilocybe cubensis*. Let us add the possibility of *P. cubensis* mushrooms being cultivated indoors by the early Alchemists is a fascinating one, and it begs the question of whether or not they (the mushrooms) could also have been cultivated outdoors. Continuing this line of inquiry, the mysterious homunculus – that tiny, humanoid, golem-like being purported to be created by the Alchemists from horse dung – immediately springs to mind.

While we may have here revealed a portion of the many mysteries of Our Lady Alchymia, it is regretful that said mysteries must necessarily be unveiled only by degrees. For, the mysteries may be exposed in their totality only upon the Alchemist's correct application of this stone of the wise. The wonders which accompany the lapis philosophorum upon its proper application are veritably beyond the mind's capacity to conceive; beyond the tongue's ability to speak. Truly, they are ineffable in the fullest sense of the word. To quote once more from E.A. Hitchcock anonymous commentator,

> "And such are the Wonders of Heaven displayed, that when they do shew forth their Glory their Virtue is not within the Power of Man to speak, for such spoke Paul who was caught up unto the Third Heaven where he saw that which cannot be spoken, nor imagined. Its Vitality is like a Tincture which doth elevate the Mind to sublimity of Thought, greater than can be imagined."[12]

---

11 Libavius, Andreas. *Images of Alchemical Apparatus.*
12 Privately communicated by Clark Heinrich

BEFORE THE WASSONS
PART I: MAGIC MUSHROOMS IN NORTH AMERICA

Living in the Deep South where they grow wild in virtually every grain-fed cattle field, my brother and I first began foraging *Psilocybe cubensis* mushrooms in our early teens. Once while hunting for mushrooms in a field next to our paternal grandmother's home in Senatobia, Mississippi, we were mortified to discover that our rather square and straight-shooting uncle had been watching us from the house as we picked. My brother and I quickly ditched the harvested specimens and walked reluctantly to where our uncle stood waiting. To our surprise, he wasn't reprimanding in the least. Rather, he was grinning widely as he chided us: "Boys, you two are jus' like ya great-great grandaddy Daugherty; ya grandmama's grandaddy. You'd catch him er' morn at the crack of dawn, walkin' them there cow fields, lookin' for mushrooms and herbs. He was a healer, ya know?" "A healer!?" I exclaimed inquisitively. "That's right" he answered. "He trained with a Native American; Chickasaw or Choctaw. I can't recall which. You'll have to ask ya grandmama."

Of course, I have no way of knowing if the mushrooms that my great-great Grandfather Daugherty was allegedly harvesting were actually *P. cubensis*. Nor do I know if the Choctaw or Chickasaw tribes even possess(ed) a knowledge of the visionary properties of coprophilic psilocybin mushrooms. I recount this anecdote only as a means of raising the question of whether or not psilocybin mushrooms could have been known to certain esoteric circles in North America prior to the publication of the Wassons' article in *Life Magazine* in May of 1957.

Ethan Allen Hitchcock, who died in Georgia in August of 1870, was a career United States Army officer that served as a major general during the American Civil War. He was also an avid student of and commentator upon alchemy. A note discovered in the back flyleaf of a copy of Hitchcock's classic study *Remarks Upon Alchemy* (1857) and communicated to us privately by Clark Heinrich reads:

> *"the Secret of our Stone…shall shew itself forth as though it bloomed sweetly upon the dunghill. And if you shall ask me what*

it resembles – I shall say to you that it lives and is to be found in the likeness and form of many things in Nature. For it can be as the Moon as has been said – If they say the Moon is blue, we must believe that it is true. – But this only if molested, for the colour of the Moon is white in its naturalistic State."

What other than the *Psilocybe cubensis* mushroom meets the criteria of being at once a living thing in nature that, in addition to 'blooming' upon dung, also appears as the moon, i.e. round and pale, unless the same has been "molested," in which case it then turns blue?

Psilocybe cubensis is a coprophilic mushroom meaning that it can only subsist upon the dung of certain species. Its psychoactive constituents are a pair of powerful compounds termed psilocin and psilocybin, first synthesized by Swiss chemist Albert Hofmann and brought to the attention of the Western world by amateur mycologist R. Gordon Wasson. Although pale in its undisturbed state, the *Psilocybe cubensis* mushroom has the unique characteristic of staining blue when bruised or broken. This reaction is due to the oxidation of the psilocin and psilocybin contained in the mushroom, and serves as an easy identifier for inclined fungus foragers. Psilocin and psilocybin are also present in the mushroom *Psilocybe semilanceata*; the famous so-called "liberty cap."

In 1783, Sir William "Oriental" Jones, Jr., after whom the character Indiana Jones was modeled, received a letter from Benjamin Franklin telling him about the *Libertas Americana* ("American freedom") medal. As Franklin's letter implies, he and Jones likely discussed the proposed medal while in Paris. Franklin wrote, "The engraving of my medal, which you know was projected before the peace, is but just finished... You will see that I have profited by some of your ideas, and adopted the mottoes you were so kind to furnish." The following excerpt comes from Mike Crowley's fascinating paper *Oriental Jones and the Medal of Freedom*:

> *"The obverse of this medal shows the head of 'Miss Liberty' against a background of a liberty cap on a pole. The red, woolen pileus ('liberty cap'), a cap worn by freed slaves in ancient Rome, was a popular symbol for 'liberty' and in the colonies a cap on a pole signified defiance of the British. Another meaning of pileus was introduced in the middle of the 18th century: it is the scientific term for the cap of a mushroom. As members of the Royal Society, the premier scientific body of their time, both Franklin and Jones would have been exposed to the latest in technical terminology. Another term introduced about the same time as pileus was stipe, the botanical term*

for a mushroom's stalk or stem. The original meaning of the Latin stipe was 'pole' or 'stake,' so we may assume that Jones, fluent in Latin, would make the connection between the American symbol of cap-on-pole with pileus-on-stipe. Furthermore, as an active member of the Royal Society, it would be surprising if he did not connect this with the recently coined terminology of mushroom anatomy.

The proportions of Franklin's medal and its beautifully executed bust of Liberty have made this one of the most sought-after coins in the world. However, in contrast to his naturalistic depiction of Liberty, the cap-on-a-pole that leans diagonally behind her is extremely stylized. The cap, in particular, is unlike any other representation of this symbolic headgear and is unlike the coinage subsequently based on the medal. Rather than falling on limp folds, as cloth should, it is smooth, rigid, and symmetrical about the pole. To be frank, it bears an uncanny resemblance to the 'liberty cap' (Psilocybe semilanceata) mushroom, not just in its shape and the proportions of cap and stem but also in that it appears to mimic the mushroom's 'acute umbo' and 'striated margin,' both of which are distinguishing features of this species.

All mushrooms of the Psilocybe genus have an umbo, a small bump at the center of the cap, but P. semilanceata is notable for its particularly pointed bump (an acute umbo). The cap of a P. semilanceata mushroom also has a translucent band around its outermost edge allowing its gills to be visible as a band of vertical stripes. This is called a 'translucent-striate margin.' Though small, this 'highly to extremely potent' entheogen forms extensive colonies in meadows of rye grass and grows in great profusion on the green hills of Wales, Jones' homeland." [1]

It is notable that while Franklin is known to have held little to no interest in laboratory alchemy, in 1773 Samuel Danforth, who served as judge and chief justice in Massachusetts for over three decades, wrote to his long-time friend Benjamin Franklin offering to send him a piece of the legendary *philosopher's stone*.[2] Like Hitchcock's "Stone" and Jones' "liberty cap," is it possible that Danforth's substance could have been a type of psilocybin mushroom?

In 1779, artist John Folwell crafted a chair, now known as the "Rising Sun

---

1   Crowley, Mike. *Secret Drugs in Buddhism.*
2   Stavish, Mark. *The History of Alchemy in America.*

Armchair," for the newly elected president of a fledgling nation. From May, 25 to September, 17 of 1787, Folwell's chair was occupied by George Washington for the entire duration of the Grand Convention at Philadelphia.[3] Now housed at the Independence National Historical Park in Philadelphia, Pennsylvania, on the back of Washington's Rising Sun Armchair is depicted a golden rising sun surmounted by what appears to be a parasol, also in gold. However, there is something admittedly enigmatic about this particular parasol. Parasol is a French word derived from the Italian *parasole; para* – 'to protect against,' and *sole* – 'the sun.' How odd then that the parasol depicted on Washington's Rising Sun Armchair should be shown as being elevated *above* the sun, as opposed to below it. This is not at all where one would normally expect to see a parasol depicted. Indeed, Folwell's carving appears to be a veritable rebus. Additionally, the parasol carved by Folwell upon Washington's armchair is highly stylized. For, it features the very same 'translucent-striate margin' – the band of vertical stripes found upon the *pileus* of a *P. semilanceata* mushroom – that we encountered on Franklin and Jones' *Libertas Americana* medallion. Could it too be an example of a psilocybin mushroom? If so, it would go far in explaining the nature of the angelic vision allegedly suffered by Washington at Valley Forge during the winter of 1777-78, the same having been recounted by one Continental soldier Anthony Sherman in an article titled *Vision of Washington*, published by *The National Tribune* in 1880.[4] A similar arrangement of a parasol being curiously situated *above* a sun can be seen in the remarkable mural painted by Allyn Cox that graces the north wall of the Memorial Hall at the George Washington Masonic Memorial in Alexandria, Virginia.

What are the implications?

---

3   Grand Lodge of Pennsylvania. *Proceedings of the Right Worshipful Freemasons of the Grand Lodge of Pennsylvania*, P. 339.
4   Bradshaw, Wesley. *George Washington's Vision*.

BEFORE THE WASSONS
PART II: MAGIC MUSHROOMS IN THE UNITED KINGDOM

Turning our attention overseas, we find that the United States is not the only country to harbor early mushroom enthusiasts. English Psychic Spiritualist Emma Hardinge Britten (1823-1899) is a perfect example. Believed by some to have been a young seeress for Masonic Rosicrucian Frederick Hockley, Britten was present at the Spiritualist meeting in America which eventually led to the creation of the Theosophical Society under Blavatsky and Olcott.[1]

Among her writings are the following telling excerpts:

> *"The arts necessary for study to the practical occultist are...a knowledge of the qualities of drugs, vapours, minerals, electricity, perfumes, fumigations, and all kinds of anaesthetics..."*[2]

> *"Drugs...(especially hashish, opium, and nitrous oxide) are useful [for achieving power and communicating with the hierarchies.] The use of Hasheesh, Napellus, Opium, the juice of the Indian Soma, or Egyptian Lotus plant, besides many other narcotics of special virtues, constitute a large portion of the preparatory exercises..."*[3]

> *"The Soma juice, hasheesh, opium, the napellus, and distillations procured from two or three species of acrid fungi, are considered the most effective narcotics appropriate for inducing the trance condition."*[4]

---

1   Mathiesen, Robert. *The Unseen Worlds of Emma Hardinge Britten: Some Chapters in the History of Western Occultism.*
2   Godwin, Joscelyn. *The Hermetic Brotherhood of Luxor: Initiatic and Historical Documents of an Order of Practical Occultism*, P. 287.
3   Deveney, John Patrick. P*aschal Beverly Randolph: A Nineteenth Century Black American Spiritualist, Rosicrucian, and Sex Magician*, P. 43.
4   Britten, William. *Art Magic, or Mundane, Sub-Mundane and Super-Mundane Spiritism*, P. 136.

What "two or three species of acrid fingi," Britten does not specify. However, the fact that she mentions more than one is significant. For, in the 19th century the only entheogenic mushroom that was known to the West was the *Amanita muscaria*, the famous *fly agaric*. Chances are that at least one of the other mushrooms to which she refers was a psilocybin mushroom, likely *Semilanceata cyanescens*, aka the *liberty cap*, a mushroom that is native to the region.

Britten was a member of a London secret society known as Orphic Circle, a group which centered itself purely upon practical occultism.[5] Moreover, she was believed by Rene Guenon to have been a member of the Hermetic Brotherhood of Luxor, another secret society whose focus was wholly on the practical side of the occult.[6] Considering the fact that she and Peter Davidson, the Provincial Grand Master of the Northern and Eastern Sections of the H.B.L., shared a keen interest in the magical and mystical virtues of plants, this may have indeed been the case.

Around the same time, we discover related accounts in the UK from Alphonse Louis Constant, better known as Eliphas Levi. He says in *The History of Magic*:

> *"The progress of Magnetism will one day lead to the discovery of the absorbent properties of the Mistletoe of the Oak. We shall then know the secret of those spongy excrescences which draw their unused surplus from trees, and surcharge themselves from their tinctures and saps; the Mushrooms, the Truffles, the Galls of trees... Then we will no more laugh at Paracelsus..."*[7]

Of course, the oak tree is a common host to the mycorrhizal fungus f*ly agaric*. While not a psilocybin mushroom, the fact that Levi alludes to an entheogenic fungus at all we feel is worthy of mention. The reference to Paracelsus is telling, too, as the Alchemistic healer actually refers to an agaric in his writings.[8]

Again, in A.E. Waite's *The Mysteries of Magic: A Digest of the Writings of Eliphas Levi* (1886) we read:

> *"In the middle ages, the necromancers...compounded philtres and ointments...; they mixed aconite, belladonna, and poisonous fungi... Their howlings were heard at great distances, and the belated traveler fancied that legions of phantoms were issuing from the*

---

5   Deveney, John Patrick. *Paschal Beverly Randolph*, P. 35.
6   *Ibid.*, P. 259.
7   Waite, Arthur Edward. *The History of Magic by Eliphas Levi*, P. 185.
8   Weeks, Andrew. *Paracelsus*, P. 32.

> earth; the very trees assumed in his eyes affrighting shapes, flaming orbs seemed glaring in the thickets, while frogs of the marshes appeared to repeat hoarsely the words of the Sabbath. It was the mesmerism of hallucination and the contagion of madness. [They] extracted the poisonous and narcotic humour from fungi."[9]

Replete with aural and visual hallucinations, morphing, menacing phantasms, disembodied orbs of light, and even frogs chanting the liturgy of the Church, this latter account appears to be far more telling of psilocybin, as opposed to muscimol, intoxication. Further, one wonders if Levi is not here speaking from personal experience.

Returning to Paracelsus, we read in A.E. Waite's *The Hermetic and Alchemical Writings of Paracelsus*:

> "The natural mumia should be compounded out of three chief antimonies so that the foreign microcosm should govern the physical body, whether by means of the element water or by means of its metals, salts, etc., or otherwise by means of the element of earth, as by its herbs and boleti, or in tereniabin or nostoch. For all these are mansions of the supercelestial things."[10]

In response to this Waite adds:

> "Boleti. Boletus is a mushroom. Bolitus is the same as Bolbiton, i.e., the excrement of oxen. These explanations will, perhaps, not throw much light on the use of the term by Paracelsus."[11]

Why would Waite wish to draw connections between a mushroom and the excrement of oxen in regard to Paracelsus? Does he mean to insinuate that, like Britten and Levi, Paracelsus perhaps knew something of entheogenic coprophilic fungi?

Clearly both Britten and Levi, and even perhaps Paracelsus and Waite, were not ignorant of the psychedelic potential of certain plants and mushrooms. Moreover, their accounts show us that the use of special narcotics and entheogens were not foreign to the practices of magic and mysticism. While psilocybin-containing mushrooms were not brought to the greater attention of

---

9 Waite, Arthur Edward. *The Mysteries of Magic: A Digest of the Writings of Eliphas Levi*, pp. 135-174.
10 De Laurence, L.W. *The Hermetic and Alchemical Writings of Aureolus Phillippus Theophrastus Bombast of Hohenheim, Called Paracelsus, the Great by A.E. Waite*, P. 342.
11 *Ibid.* P. 357.

the Western world until the publication of the Wassons' ground-breaking article in *LIFE Magazine* in 1957, it is our strong suspicion that these phenomenal fungi may well have been known to certain secretive circles long prior. These two short papers are by no means a final proof of such. They are a meager start. The case is still very much an open one, and we encourage future generations to investigate the problem further.

SUKARAMADDAVA AND PSILOCYBIN

According to legend, the last meal of the Buddha, the same of which effectively killed him, was something called *sukaramaddava*, meaning *boar's delight*, and was given to him by the village goldsmith.[1] As Wasson has speculated in his book *Persephone's Quest: Entheogens and the Origins of Religion*, sukaramaddva is a likely allusion to a sclerotia or truffle of some variety. For, truffles are a favorite food among wild boar, and specially trained pigs are employed to this day in order to locate these culinary delicacies.

Psilocybe Mexicana, for example, is one species of psychedelic mushroom that is prone to producing sclerotia. In Amsterdam, where psilocybin-containing sclerotia are not controlled, these are known as *Philosopher's Stone Truffles* and have in recent times become all the rage since psilocybin-containing fruiting bodies were outlawed there a number of years ago.[2] Even *Tuber melanosporum*, the so-called black truffle, arguably the most sought after delicacy of the culinary world, is possessed of a certain "bliss molecule" called *anandamide* which, according to enthusiasts, offers a THC-like high.[3]

Sclerotia are formed by arresting the life-cycle of sclerotia-prone mushroom species before they're able to produce fruiting bodies. This makes sclerotia cultivation significantly easier than the delicate cultivation of fruiting bodies as, up until the sclerotia are harvested, the production process never goes beyond the inoculation stage.

Mike Crowley, author of the currently unpublished manuscript *Secret Drugs of Buddhism*, has privately communicated to us that a further proof of the identification of *sukaramaddava* as a psilocybin-containing mushroom lies in the fact that it was offered to the Buddha in an attempt to save his life. For, the Buddha was suffering from dysentery. According to Vedic scriptures, *Soma* is said to confer upon its drinker the gift of immortality. As McKenna observes in his classic *Psilocybin Mushroom Grower's Guide*, in 1984 heterodox Bengali Hindus announced the identification of the Vedic intoxicant *Soma* as

---

1   Wasson, R. Gordon. *Persephone's Quest: Entheogens and the Origins of Religion*, P. 117-127.
2   Morris, Hamilton. *Hamilton and the Philosopher's Stone*.
3   Fleming, Nic. *Truffles contain 'bliss' molecule*.

being *Psilocybe cubensis*, one of the many psilocybin-containing fungus species.[4] What better way to reverse the Buddha's ill fate than a purported elixir of immortality?

Considered allegorically, on the other hand, the story of the Buddha's demise may not refer to an actual death at all, but rather to the so-called ego death (comparable to the Buddhist concept of *Anata* or No-Self) which is commonly reported by users of psilocybin. This effect is believed to be caused by the silencing of the brain's 'central hub,' resulting in a decreased sense of self as well as in the "hyperconnection" of certain portions of the brain which do not normally communicate.[5]

Whatever the case of *sukaramaddava* and the death of the Buddha may be, almost two-thousand five hundred years after his death, one cannot help but be repeatedly amazed by the persistent relevance of the Buddha's life and teachings.

---

4   Oss, O.T. *Psilocybin Mushroom Grower's Guide*, P. 66.
5   Ghose, Tia. *Magic Mushrooms Create a Hyperconnected Brain*.

APPENDIX

DIMETHYLTRYPTAMINE EXPERIENCE REPORTS

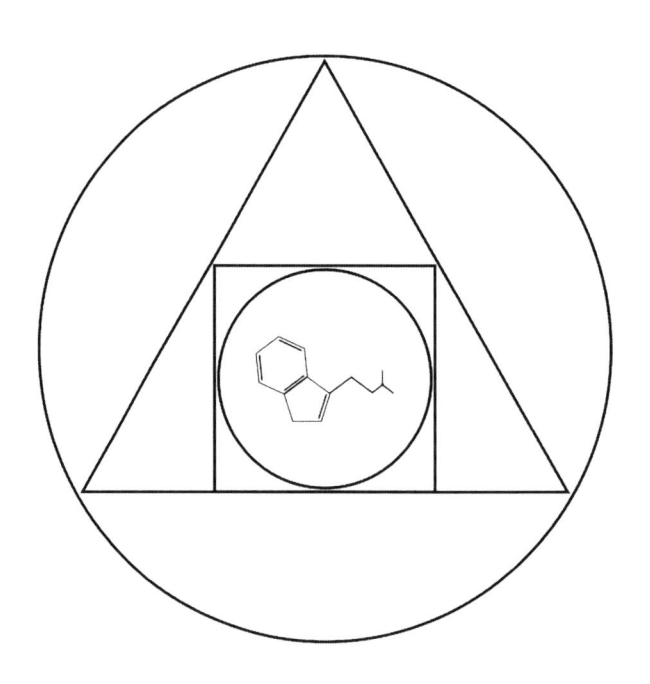

DMT EXPERIENCE REPORT NO. 1

Subject: American male, age 33
Substance: N,N-DMT, smoked
Setting: Ritualistic

It was midnight on a stormy Bicycle Day in 2015. I loaded my pipe with some DMT crystals that had been prepared by a close associate. Immediately after the first, small toke, paranoia ensued and I became conscious of what appeared to be a large crystal centipede that, while unseen, seemed to be somewhere in the room with me. Putting this out of my mind for the moment, I took a second toke and, for reasons I cannot explain, before I even exhaled, I found myself walking outside onto my second story balcony. The next thing I recall is seeing an enormous flash before my eyes, accompanied with the sensation that I was being electrocuted. Had I been struck by lightning? My body was stiff with paralysis as I watched the railing of my balcony recede from me as though I was floating. Just then, the sky appeared to open, revealing an exquisite honeycomb palace or temple, mosque-like, in the heavens. Its appearance was as molten liquid gold. All over the surface, I noticed, were undulating Sri yantras which rippled, interpenetrating, as though a handful of pebbles had been thrown into still water. All the sudden, while engrossed in these geometries, I became aware of an insect-like buzzing that was quickly encompassing my entire being. As the sound increased in volume and intensity, it became clear that this terrifying, inhuman, growl of a hum was being projected from my own open mouth – how, I cannot say. It was a sound which I had never-before produced, and have never since been able to reproduce. The shock of this noise faded when it dawned on me that from the palace in the sky was emanating what I can only describe as a hive mind. There was a sense of being locked in to this hive intelligence as though my mind were some conscious appendage. At this point I directed my gaze downward and, to my shock, there stood what looked to be some Aztec or Mayan death deity. He towered some twenty-five feet tall. His head was as a skull, framed by what to me suggested the Mayan calendar. In every arm of this menacing figure was held aloft a different weapon, each threatening me with the warning that should I progress any further it would mean the death of my physical body. Before I could make up my mind as to which would be preferable – a return to waking consciousness or the prospect of exploring the unknown – I found myself erect on my balcony, standing with my arms outstretched in the form of a cross; my mouth agape and eyes directed at the place in the sky where there once shone a glistening palace-temple. The decision to reintegrate into waking consciousness had apparently been made for me, and for the next hour or so I was pervaded with the worrisome yet exhilarating sense that I had successfully trespassed into a territory which man was not meant or expected to experience – at least not while living.

DMT EXPERIENCE REPORT NO. 2

Subject: American female, age 31
Substance: N,N-DMT, smoked
Setting: Casual

> *I am an experimental sort of user, using unusual substances maybe only once or very seldom. I had been wanting to try DMT after reading and hearing about in and after watching a documentary on the subject. My roommate at the time had offered only a "half dose" for me to try. I assumed it would be enough to have an experience, but not quite enough for an 'out of body' experience. He offered a dark brown resin tar to smoke. It didn't smell like anything I'd encountered, quite pungent. I heated the resin, inhaled the fumes in long breaths and held in as long as I could before exhaling. I video recorded myself, although the video is lost and nothing unusual or notable happened physically. I immediately laid on my bed in my tiny bohemian style bedroom. The bedroom room was only wide enough to fit my bed and with just enough space for my computer desk and four feet of walking space. Naturally there were only outlets for light on the desk side of the room which always left my bed side very dark. Once I laid down, I immediately felt a rush of energy and butterflies to the stomach, so to speak. I noticed the lite side of the room became very dark, and the bed side where I lay lite up brilliantly as if all the lights were thrown to this side of the room. I felt energized and surprisingly comfortable of my surroundings. Stress-free. I spent most of my 'trip' starring at the ceiling that had a mild texture plastered under the dull white paint. But during my experience, my surroundings were anything but dull. The white ceiling glowed with brilliant colors, and I began to see images and patterns above me taking up my entire line of vision. I was mesmerized by visions of swimming dolphins, living Egyptian motifs and scenes (as if the walls of ancient Egyptian art had come to life), and visions of a couple holding each other in embrace and love. The couple I focused on were transparent shell, seeing their veins, muscles I tissue organs and blood in movement as one kissed the other on the cheek. It reminded me of the famous artist, Alex Grey's, work. Butterflies fluttered around. Outside of the visuals, I will never forget the feeling I had of utter peace, tranquility and*

unification of my being to my surroundings. The feeling was so intense, so beautiful, it brought tears to my eyes. My 'trip' was losing momentum, and I came down back into the mundane mind. I wiped the tears from my eyes as I turned off the video, noticing only 15 minutes or so had gone by. In my assessment, it is not a 'party drug' but a tool for a quiet, meditative shamanic journey. It is something meant to be respected and used for a purpose. To this day, I do wish I had a full 'dose' and I would absolutely love to try it again.

DMT EXPERIENCE REPORT NO. 3

Subject: British male, age 44
Substance: N,N-DMT, intravenous
Setting: Clinical

I recently (2016) participated in a DMT study at my university. It was a two-arm single-blind study design, so there were two visits, spaced one week apart. One would be a placebo dose and the other an active dose. The researchers knew which was which, but the participants didn't. (Although it was pretty obvious once the active dose occurred!)

Study visit: Week One: No Effect. Presumed placebo.

Study Visit: Week Two:

Status: Definitely active dose today. Experience: Within 30 seconds of the DMT injection going in I was immediately aware of a sudden high-pitched whistling coming from behind me, in the distance below the bed. It crescendoed into a blunting sound; a phaser-like filtered muffling. Then I was suddenly enveloped from the tip of my toes to (the) top of (my) head with an intense blanket of paralyzing bodily warmth; a syrupy, yet 'dry', goo. And I was within a grid-like lattice-work of hexagonal/octagonal purply-greeny-blue sea of shifting geometric shapes; undulating, morphing. But I was not 'in' this scene in a physical bodily sense. Rather I 'was' this environment, I was part of this matrix. It was an intense sense of boundary-less 'sameness' within a shifting landscape. This experience lasted for around five minutes - though time itself was fluid and tunneled, so it was difficult to be sure. The matrix landscape slowly faded to a closed-eye, blotchy orange visual field (I was blindfolded throughout, with eyes shut) and my sense of physical body-centeredness returned. But I was still paralyzed; limp and dissociated like a puppet. I was aware of shapes moving around in my peripheral vision, there was a presence of others. This lasted for around twenty minutes, gradually fading. Meanwhile the study team continued to draw regular blood samples from the needle in my other arm. After around thirty minutes from the injection

I removed the eyeshades and they stopped the EEG recording. I was left with a mild, opiate-like, sedation for around another twenty minutes and by one hour was completely back to baseline mental state. It was neither ecstatic or frightening, but rather, curious, intriguing and peculiar, in a benign way. There was no afterglow. And no clear mystical-spiritual element to the experience. But a definite other-worldliness about it.

No contact with entities.

DMT EXPERIENCE REPORT NO. 4

Subject: American male, age 28
Substance: 5-MeO-DMT, smoked
Setting: Casual

About 7 years ago, when I was 21, I had my first experience with 5-MeO-DMT. It was around 8pm when me and my wife were sitting at our music room table. We had recently scored some supposedly very high quality deems, powdery and yellow brown in color. We had been smoking dank all night and decided it was time for our first deems trip. She asked if I wouldn't mind tripping first since she was skeptical and of course I agreed. I put a small bud in the bottom of my bowl to block the hole up. Put approximately .05g, which the seller had told me was around half a dose. I took one deep pull while barely touching the flame to the powder. I remember the first thing I noticed was the awful taste like the way rotten eggs smell. I held it as long as I felt comfortable and expelled the smoke. I didn't feel anything immediately at all so seconds later I decided I was really going to rip it. So I put the lighter to it and while I was inhaling for the second time the room began to breath. By the time I had remembered I was still holding a couple lungs full of DMT smoke I closed my eyes and the most extravagant and lush visuals filled the back of my eye lids. I decided to enjoy them for a few seconds. What I would see when I opened them I would never forget. On my clear glass music room table was the gigantic blueprint of a magnificent city with a beautiful skyline as if it were all drawn up by some God like contractor on blue paper. Every building drawn like a white lines hologram on glassy clear blue background. I immediately closed my eyes again and rubbed them vigorously. When I opened them, the same beatific city was still there. Only this time I could stand up and walk around my table observing every intimate detail of what I would call the most beautiful place in the universe. I stood walking around for the next two minutes at least until I rested back on the couch. I then saw it, in the most majestic manor, slowly fade away as my conscience slowly drifted back into reality. All I could mutter to my wife was please don't be afraid of this. Please you have to see what I have seen. Not understanding that everyone's trip will always be different I urged her to smoke it which actually frightened her a bit. After about 6-8 minutes I was finally realizing that what had happened to me would stay clear in my mind forever and that nothing on this earth could ever take that experience from me and that certainly nothing could take its place in not only my mind but my whole being. Her experience was quite different. She toked easily on it once, afraid of where she might go. She had good visuals and her experience was enjoyable. But me, I had a life changing experience in a matter of minutes.

DMT EXPERIENCE REPORT NO. 5

Subject: American female, age 34
Substance: N,N-DMT, smoked
Setting: Casual

Some four years ago I was living in downtown Tupelo and the opportunity arose for me to try changa. I hadn't done DMT in a number of years, and the last time I attempted it was less than memorable. I was alone with my husband and one of his Brother Masons. My husband loaded me a bowl of DMT-infused passionflower on cannabis. It wasn't until I took my 3rd toke that I knew I was well on my way. My 'self' travelled fast out of the top of my head and immediately all of my vision was taken up by vibrant colors and intense patterns. The 'machine elves' I had always heard McKenna talk about were there, distracting me with their benignly menacing dancing. They were all riding bicycles in circles which created these rotating squares, all of which were also spinning in repeat patterns. Their action seemed to be the driving energy behind the movement of the world; of all human experience – almost like they were running a generator on the astral plane. They were hypnotizing and seemed to be saying to me, "See all these pretty colors? Look at what we can do! All of our tricks!" I felt caught up in their incessant pattern making. I became part of it. It was almost like being in a moving, 3D Alex Grey painting. Our movements were generating this other-worldly music that I could literally feel in my head and seemed to perpetuate the patterns vibrating in colors. There was a prevailing sense that I had been in this place before. I also knew there was much more beyond this veil of color and pattern-making. Expecting and wanting to go further, I inquired "Is this it?" About that time the veil of reality dissolved completely and I was suddenly in what I can only describe as the 'white room,' a type of waiting room I find myself in only on high doses of psychedelics. There is no 'thing' and no sense of 'self' in that room. It's rather disconcerting!

I should mention that, before I began smoking, I requested that my husband select some music which he thought might be appropriate for a DMT trip. Being the production-oriented musician that he is, his first choice was The Beach Boys' "Smile," a record which at the time he had been playing often. This was, for me, a terrible choice. In any other setting it might have been preferable. But, the music wound up having a negative influence on my experience. Apparently, the point in the song "Heroes and Villains" when a voice announces "You're under arrest!" coincided with the point in my trip when I went into the "white room." It was at that point in the experience, I later learned, that my face went slack and I was noticeably disassociated.

As the "white room" dissolved and reality began to slowly return, there was an overwhelming physical sensation that I was wrapped in warm, thick liquid, like honey. I thought I may have peed on myself and keep checking to see, but I had not. As I looked around the room, I saw my husband in full patterns and colors sitting and smiling and breathing the room in and out. He appeared to me as the new Laughing, full- bellied Buddha. I was sitting directly across from him and began to mimic his rhythmic breathing. I looked down at the hardwood floors and they were lines of rainbow-colored, kaleidoscopic chomping crocodiles, all going in alternate directions. As I swept my hands across them, their images swirled and rippled like I was moving my hands across water. This continued until I was completely back to reality.

DMT EXPERIENCE REPORT NO. 6

Subject: American male, age 31
Substance: N,N-DMT, smoked
Setting: Casual

This experience is from the time I smoked DMT on top of dried Egyptian blue lotus flowers with my wife. Sitting in a meditative position, I smoked and closed my eyes. I remember seeing triangles; one right-side-up on top, and one upside-down on the bottom. They were lit up with many colors that were changing rapidly, like a twinkling star. With closed eyes, patterns covered the 'walls' of my vision. I directed my perception upwards and saw a tribalesque sun face that appeared of South American origin. The face was almost like a face in the middle of a totem pole, at the far end of a temple. It was at that point that I realized I actually was in a temple of some sort. To my left and right there were huge Greek-style columns. I started hearing some kind of music, although I'm unsure when it began or from where it came. I cannot recall the sound of it now, but it was definitely music. I badly wanted to turn around and view the rest of the temple, but a force kept my perception directed at the sun face between the pillars. I barely recall two guards standing near the columns. Both appeared as frog or toad people. Looking at the sun, I also saw a number of archways accompanied by a large, triangular architecture that I can only describe as Greek or Roman. As I started to come back to my senses, I felt a pressure in my ears as though I was under water or coming down off a mountain. Then the music stopped. Keeping my eyes closed, the scene faded into the darkness. The last thing to go were the colors. I felt a peace and a 'oneness' with everyone I encountered throughout the next twenty-four hours.

DMT EXPERIENCE REPORT NO. 7

Subject: American male, age 40
Substance: N,N-DMT, intravenous
Setting: Casual

Having had several successful trips from smoking N,N-DMT, I decided I'd take it to the next level and do an intravenous administration. After about the third heartbeat following the pushing of the plunger, BOOM! It was as if the Great Architect of the Universe assaulted me with trans-dimensional information. As I felt a warmth encompass my body, there came a noise, as though reality were being ripped apart. I've heard this sound before after smoking DMT, but nowhere this intense. Siren-like, I could not only hear the sound, but see and feel it.

Suddenly I found myself surrounded by fractals that seemed to pulse and flash with every heartbeat. As the noise subsided, I felt a sensation as if I were floating. I found myself hovering in front of what can only be explained as a waterfall of mercury. I pushed my 'hand' through the quicksilver to see if it was real. As soon as I pulled my 'hand' out, I felt a pressure on the back of my head, as though someone were pushing me from behind. The unseen force proceeded to push me through the waterfall and into labyrinth-like abyss of subterranean caverns. While I took flight through this endless black abyss, I began to recall repressed childhood memories. As soon as I acknowledged the memories, their flow stopped – as did my flight. I found myself in a space that was blacker than pitch, talking to myself.

At this point I seemed to have forgotten everything, including the fact that I had injected DMT. Out of nowhere the fractals returned, pulsing, and engulfed me; made me a part of them. At one point, it became so overwhelming that I wanted them to cease. The moment that thought manifested itself I found myself somewhere completely different. I was looking at myself on a different plane altogether. I noticed several beings around me that seemed to be aware of my presence. They were saying "Hey, you! You're not supposed to be in here!" I was petrified. The sensation was that I was in that place for an eternity.

Then, all the sudden, the voice of what I interpreted to be a goddess began speaking to me, reassuring me that all would be well. She was playing with my long hair, telling me sweetly that I was a good person. Oddly, there were no actual words exchanged. I remember admiring her exquisite beauty, thinking to myself that she appeared as the very essence of Mother Nature. It was a comforting embrace and I did not want to leave. What seemed like a lifetime suddenly returned to reality as I remembered it. The trip faded, and I found myself being held up from behind by my best friend. The experience all at once overwhelmed me and I began to cry. He let go of me and asked if I was okay, saying that he had to grab me because, while on the drug, I began walking about, babbling nonsensically.

It took me months to get grounded from the experience. To this day I find myself thinking of it often.

DMT EXPERIENCE REPORT NO. 8

Subject: American male, age 32
Substance: N,N-DMT, smoked
Setting: Casual

> *I sat down with the pipe in as close to total darkness as I could, attempting to ease the anxiety that always accompanies the unknown. This would be my first real experience with DMT. I remember the veil getting thin, and then I saw it. It was like an extreme close-up of some continually-morphing, ever-cycling creature with textures, hieroglyphs, colors, and shapes of ancient pictographs and native iconography. There were hieroglyphs and cuneiform in relief, as well as totem pole faced along with Mayan symbols and Native American color schemes. It was so much so fast that I could not grasp it all. There was a recurring symbol that kept manifesting. It looked like the top of a totem pole and was the profile of a bird's head. The entire scene seemed to back away from me at that point and allowed me to get a good look at it in all its glory. Towards the end of the trip, it struck me that whatever influenced those native cultures; whatever common thread ran through their societies, like a muse whispering into the ears of their artists and thinkers – this was that muse; some ancient fairy-like entity in an alternate dimension; a living, breathing representation of all these native cultures and languages. It was such a profound insight into our history as a people that I openly wept when the vision began to fade, and the veil returned once more, like an iron curtain separating me from the 'other.' If I had ten more hits of DMT in front of me at the time, I would have smoked all of it right then, just to get back to that place where all linguistic ambitions and the living, breathing hopes and dreams of dead culture still exist; still roaming the astral in search of a worthy candidate for initiation!*

DMT EXPERIENCE REPORT NO. 9

Subject: American male, age 33
Substance: Psilocybin, ingested + N,N-DMT, smoked
Setting: Ritualistic

It was Easter Sunday, 2013. Having participated in Lent, the celebration of Holy Week had commenced, including a participation in the Ancient and Accepted Scottish Rite, Southern Jurisdiction's Ceremony of Remembrance and Renewal. Following the Mystic Banquet, I returned with my wife to our place of abode, where we partook of a mystic banquet of a different kind: ten dried grams of highly potent Psilocybe cubensis mushroom powder. These were mushrooms that we had harvested ourselves from a local cow field, so I knew them to be of formidable potency.

I prepared the fungus a day prior by infusing the powder in a bottle of port wine, to which I added a splash of orange juice, creating a sort of psychedelic sangria. The citric acid also assists in the infusion process. Having strained out the plant matter using a fine cheese cloth, I transferred the elixir into a decanter, put on Coil's Musick to Play in the Dark Vols. 1 & 2, and poured us each a glass.

The first effects I noted were from the alcohol, but not long into my second or third glass, I began to sense the first waves of psilocybin intoxication wash over my being. My wife imbibed about a third of the bottle. I finished the rest. Relaxing on our bed, the effects came on fully and were much stronger than either of us anticipated.

Sprawled in the silent darkness, I saw out of my peripheral vision a colorful Native American-looking bird, each feather of which was a painted arrow. As it flew across my vision, in its wake it brought the entire universe trailing behind, as if its flight was unzipping reality from nothingness. Out of this starry galaxy approached an image; a giant, blue, crystalline skull. Its appearance was as a faceted sapphire, as though it had been carved from a gemstone. Hovering above me, the skull proceeded to open its enormous mouth and vomit a waterfall of oceans and jewels into my soul.

At that point my wife and I began to make love. It was an intense rollercoaster of sensual bliss for the both of us. And, we wouldn't know it until six weeks later, but it was during that blissful union that we conceived our youngest son, B. His due date, we would learn, I might add, would be Christmas day. It is as Aleister Crowley wrote in Agape vel Liber C vel Azoth, "Thus at Easter is the Crucifixion or Copulation, and nine months later is the Birth of the Child."

My emotions and mind were keyed up to an incredible degree at this point. I decided to retire to my study where I proceeded to load my oil burner pipe with a generous amount of N,N-DMT that had been prepared for me by a colleague. Smoking alone, I recall taking toke after toke, all the way up to nine hits. Previously, I had fully blasted off on this same batch after only three hits. But, for some reason – perhaps because many of my receptors were already occupied with psilocybin – I was able to keep smoking and smoking, the visions growing more and more vivid with each inhalation.

After the ninth toke, I found myself on a lonely planet in the furthest reaches of space. Stationed on this planet was a giant reptilian brain covered by a glass dome. This brain, I knew, was the mind which thought up the entire universe. From it began to protrude a number of tentacle-like extensions, like the appendages of an octopus, all of which were conscious and possessed of their own minds. One by one, each tentacle devoured another, and every one that was consumed produce two more. As I observed the one Will branch off into multiple smaller wills, all of which ate and mated with one another in order to multiply their number, it dawned on me that what I was seeing was a symbolic representation of Arthur Schopenhauer's philosophy. It was profoundly inspiring.

At that moment, the entire scene exploded into another. I found myself looking at a humongous hermaphroditic hominid goat, not unlike Eliphas Levi's depiction of Baphomet or the drawing of the Devil card in the Marseille Tarot deck. It was composed wholly of colorful, kaleidoscopic geometry, continually morphing and shifting, but all the while maintaining its bestial shape. From its teeth hung a giant, scaly snake which, though the goat chewed perpetually, was not destroyed. This act of the-goat-forever-chewing-the-snake,

I knew, somehow sustained creation. It was baffling to behold.

Below this gigantic scene was a row of turtles, all spinning and flipping in unison. I watched this curious dance until the vision faded and I found myself sitting on the floor of my study. No more than twenty minutes had passed.

DMT EXPERIENCE REPORT NO. 10

Subject: American male, age 30
Substance: N,N-DMT, smoked
Setting: Ritualistic

There were four of us under the stairs in a storage closet where I used to record music and perform magical rites. The space was large enough for us all to sit cross-legged on the cement floor. I believe three out of we four had never tripped on DMT before, but that is precisely why we had convened. We must have decided to meet at my home because of this very room. Having no windows and being quite large for what it was, it was the perfect man-made place to take such an adventure. Additionally, we were all Freemasons. So, we were all four of like mind and intention, to be sure.

After fellowshipping upstairs, settling our nerves with a whiskey drink, we descended into the dark room. We sat on the floor in the shape of an oblong square. The eldest Frater noted that we were all Freemasons and thus proposed that we should "open Lodge." After several minutes, our virtual Lodge was open and the eldest of the four moved to the center of the room as we formed a triangle around him. The one experienced Frater held the pipe for him and instructed him to hit it as long as he could. He went from sitting to slowly reclining. His hand dropped, and our experienced Frater grabbed the pipe. We had a pillow waiting for the head of our transported Frater. He giggled. We sat in darkness for about thirty minutes. Then, he sat up and spoke. "Wow!"

When it was my turn, I too was instructed to hit the pipe until I dropped. Only, I did not fall back. I resisted. The face in front of me was the experienced Frater. It became hollow. Except for his pupils, his eyes were gone. I could literally see the walls of his eye sockets. Then, all the sudden, the room disappeared. I was then somewhere else. This realm was geometrical, colorful, organic, and tinged with a predominant orange that may have been the influence of the candle light in our midst. I heard a voice say "So, this is what you wanted, eh?" The voice was originating from within my head. Was it me asking this? Was it my Holy Guardian Angel?

Whatever it was, it was amused with my recent undertaking.

I was in the Spirit World, seeing things I was never supposed to see. I felt guilt, as though I was trespassing; like I was never going to get back home. I could hear and feel the others trying to get me to relax and recline. But, I never did. I was sitting up, but my neck and shoulders were limp. I hunched over. I was moving through this world, not unlike a soul careening to the center of the earth. It felt like it lasted thirty seconds, but I was assured it was closer to half an hour. As my eyes focused, I saw my hands curled up in my lap. I raised my right hand and it was the pure, chubby hand of an infant. I stared at it in disbelief. I thought that I had just been born, but could still remember my previous life before I 'died' under the stairs, as though it were a previous incarnation. The fear had dissolved into awe and my hand had returned to normal. Afterward, my Fratres all laughed saying "yeah, man, you were locked in on your hand like it was the most amazing thing you'd ever laid your eyes on!"

We closed our virtual Lodge and crawled upstairs, probably having another stiff drink or two. It was an incredible experience and one I might do again under the right circumstances. Yet, like all things worth doing, it was an utterly terrifying experience. And, I have not had the courage to repeat the experiment. A couple years later, I came close, but chickened out mid toke. I mean, a man can only undergo so many deaths in one lifetime.

DMT EXPERIENCE REPORT NO. 11

Subject: American male, age 66
Substance: Ayahuasca
Setting: Ritualistic

The Event began at 11:00 pm on the 14th April 2016. The experience came back to objective consciousness at around 4:00 am the following day.

I will immediately have to express that the experience I had was a totally controlled experience. The nausea effect of the MAO inhibitor is an ordeal to overcome. Yet the spiritual experience far outweighs the physical discomfort.

An experience as such certainly is not something for the weak of mind, of weak heart and of soul. The visions are out of this world. Every new phase of the experience starts with the vision of the most beautiful geometric shapes and scenes with colours experienced beyond the ordinary spectrum.

When the elevation of perceptions started to kick in, I knew immediately that a most special experience was to be had. Looking at the walls I saw dimensions open up with extraordinary colour hues blending through many layers and depths. I knew I had better lay down as I wanted to be safe in whatever happens. Yet I soon realized I had full control. This was not a psychedelic uncontrolled event. I was able to at all time, within the actual experience, analyse all that transpired at every moment. In other words, I was able to fully experience in a full awakened consciousness. I was able to retain the memory of the experience most easily without difficulty. It is still clear as day.

The first shift in consciousness was felt with very high positive emotions. Everything began to look brighter in color and shadows blended most harmoniously. As I gazed ahead of me in wonderment of the extraordinary scene of colors and geometric shapes, I saw beings, people gathered all around me. I was getting annoyed as they were crowding me, blocking my view. I felt like I was in a crowded elevator. I naturally interacted with them. I asked them who they were and what did they want? They just looked ahead and ignored me. I saw no faces I recognized. In my experience a realization came upon me. I realized that each and every one of them was a certain aspect of myself as being my cares, responsibilities, commitments, problems, worries, and all that restricts me in life. It is as though such had personified themselves. With this realization, I told them that I knew who they were and that they can now leave. They dispersed giving me my space.

I got up out of bed and decided to walk around the house. I saw my house as never before. I saw my windows all stained glassed. Guards watching over me were at their posts in every room, reminding me that I am never alone. They were like angels. If I looked at them directly, they vanished. When I looked away they were there as I saw them in the corner of my eyes.

Huge and beautiful tigers were looking into the house through some of the windows. The tigers were a realization of my strengths and powers that wanted entry into my house, my consciousness. As I looked at the floor tiles in my kitchen, characters rose above them and sceneries developed. I was being entertained with much beauty and wonderment. This was the end of my first phase as a realization into a more intense consciousness opening to me.

I next entered into the black stage of the alchemical process. I started to really feel the intense nausea effect of the MAO effect and decided to go and lay down in bed again. I know that I fell asleep for a while. Then I woke up suddenly as I felt the presence of a very dark figure. I sat up on the side of my bed and instantly put the night light on. I saw a shadow figure behind me gazing down at me. I grabbed him and threw him on the ground. With my foot I pinned him down. Having full control of the experience. I had no fear whatsoever but had a sort of disgust as to why such a figure would present itself to me. Then again a realization was had. I pointed straight at him and told him I knew who he was. That he was all my vices, my dark side, my weaknesses, and all my fears. As he realized that I had recognized him, he just dissolved under my feet. I had conquered him! I laid back down and put the light out to rest. I was hoping I would fall asleep as this was a very intense experience. My heart was beating and I felt a battle won.

I may have fallen asleep again but I am not sure. Suddenly I was in full consciousness of the presence of many beings about me again. This time they were all dressed in white robes. Men and women of noble countenance were sitting on chairs along the walls of both sides of my room. They were looking at me as if they knew me and had a gaze as though they understood what I was undergoing. Some were smiling with reassurance towards me and others with sympathetic looks. Again having full control with the power of analysis within the experience itself, a sense came onto me that I had met with all that which is belonging to the divine light within me.

Having had met previously with my worldly responsibilities and cares, after which with my shadow, these events ended the 'Black Stage'. With the meeting of the purity of the beings in white, I have now entered the purification of the 'White Stage' of the alchemical process, as I have met my virtues and all the positive aspects of my being. I was now prepared for my next stage of the alchemical process.

My experience ended with arriving at the vision of the 'Peacock's Tail' stage of the alchemical process. A most beautiful vision of colourful streamers hanging from infinite space above through an infinite area extending endlessly to depths in front and all around me. I saw space as never before. A most beautiful Christmas tree appeared with all its beautiful decorations and colours. Seeing it, I was filled with ecstasy and an immense emotion of love and of beauty. It was absolutely wonderful that I was able to almost instantly recognize this elevated emotion. The vision of this Christmas tree transported me back to my childhood emotions where I had the same ecstatic feeling as when I was two or three years old having seen my first Christmas tree. It was a memory recall with all its intense childhood emotional feeling. I experienced a sort of a rebirth in feeling and having the consciousness of the child I once was, with all the wonderments the child I once was had. It was a reawakening into a new state of spirituality encompassing all the positive energetic healing vibrations that such a rejoicing youthful experience brings along with it.

This entire spiritual voyage lasted about 7 hours. Sometimes I just got up and walked around my house as everything in it was extraordinarily beautiful. The visions lasted a good 4 hours before they subsided, after which the experience was followed by 2 hours of peaceful, silent contemplation, enjoying my new found energies. I just sat in silence, feeling my inner energies ebb and flow. It was truly spiritually most solemn. I had entered a metaphysical and mystical silence of such an intensity that I was totally engulfed in an absolute peace of self. It was truly a healing experience.

Even today colors are more vivid, feelings are heightened and my dreams are more intense. Meditations are enhanced and metaphysical energies are so much more easily generated. Recently, I read that a doctor is healing severe alcoholic and drug addicts with such DMT journeys. I am not surprised. There is a most beautiful light in us all, it just needs to be awakened from our dormant consciousness of it.

FURTHER READING

FURTHER READING ON ENTHEOGENS

Archaic Revival by Terence McKenna
Be Here Now by Ram Dass
Cannabis and the Soma Solution by Chris Bennett
Center of the Cyclone by John C. Lilly
DMT: The Spirit Molecule by Rick Strassman
DMT and the Soul of Prophesy by Rick Strassman
Food of the Gods by Terence McKenna
Heaven and Hell by Aldous Huxley
Info-Psychology by Timothy Leary
Liber 420 by Chris Bennett
LSD by Otto Snow
LSD: My Problem Child by Albert Hofmann
Magic Mushrooms in Religion and Alchemy by Clark Heinrich
Mushrooms, Myth and Mithras by Carl A.P. Ruck
Mystery School in Hyperspace by Graham St. John
Persephone's Quest by R. Gordon Wasson
Pharmacotheon by Jonathan Ott
PIHKAL by Alexander Shulgin
Plants of the Gods by Richard Evans Schultes
Programming and Metaprogramming in the Human Biocomputer by John C. Lilly
Psilocybin Mushrooms of the World by Paul Stamets
Sacred Vine of the Spirits by Ralph Metzner
Secret Drugs of Buddhism by Mike Crowley
Sex, Drugs, and Magick by Robert Anton Wilson
Soma: Divine Mushroom of Immortality by R. Gordon Wasson
Some Simple Tryptamines by K. Trout
The Apples of Apollo by Carl A.P. Ruck
The Antipodes of the Mind by Benny Shanon
The Cosmic Serpent by Jeremy Narby
The Doors of Perception by Aldous Huxley
The Effluents of Deity by Carl A.P. Ruck

FURTHER READING ON ENTHEOGENS

The Encyclopedia of Psychoactive Plants by Christian Ratsch
The Game of Life by Timothy Leary
The Mystery of Manna by Dan Merkur
The Psilocybin Solution by Simon G. Powell
The Psychedelic Experience by Timothy Leary
The Road to Eleusis by R. Gordon Wasson
The Sacred Mushroom and the Cross by John M. Allegro
The Toad of Dawn by Octavio Rettig Hinojosa
The Witches' Ointment by Thomas Hatsis
TIHKAL by Alexander Shulgan
True Hallucinations by Terence McKenna

FURTHER READING ON FREEMASONRY

A Bridge to Light by Rex Hutchens
Albert Pike's Esoterika by Arturo de Hoyos
Albert Pike's Masonic Formulas and Rituals by Arturo de Hoyos
Albert Pike's Morals and Dogma by Arturo de Hoyos
Allegorical Conversations by Arturo de Hoyos
Ancient Masonry by C.C. Zain
Cracking the Freemasons Code by Robert L.D. Cooper
E.A. Handbook by J.S.M. Ward
F.C. Handbook by J.S.M. Ward
Freemasonry by Mark Stavish
Freemasonry and Its Ancient Mystic Rites by C.W. Leadbeater
Freemasonry and the Ancient Gods by J.S.M. Ward
Freemasonry's Royal Secret by Arturo de Hoyos
Light on Masonry by Arturo de Hoyos
Lodge and the Craft by Rollin C. Blackmer
Lost Rites by David Harrison
Mackey's Revised Encyclopedia of Freemasonry by H.L. Haywood
Masonic Orthodoxy by Jean-Marie Ragon
M.M. Handbook by J.S.M. Ward
Observing the Craft by Andrew Hammer
Scottish Rite Ritual Monitor and Guide by Arturo de Hoyos
Signs and Symbols by George Oliver
Stellar Theology and Masonic Astrology by Robert Hewitt Brown
Symbolism in Craft Freemasonry by Colin Dyer
Symbolism of Freemasonry by Albert G. Mackey
The Alchemical Keys to Masonic Ritual by Timothy Hogan
The Arcane Schools by John Yarker
The Book of the Words by Albert Pike
The Encyclopedia of Freemasonry by Albert G. Mackey
The Genesis of Freemasonry by David Harrison
The Key to Solomon's Key Lon Milo DuQuette

FURTHER READING ON FREEMASONRY

The Lost Keys of Freemasonry by Manly P. Hall
The Masonic Initiation by W.L. Wilmshurst
The Masonic Magician by Philippa Faulks
The Mason's Words by Robert G. Davis
The Meaning of Masonry by W.L. Wilmshurst
The Most Secret Mysteries by Arturo de Hoyos
The Way of the Craftsman by W. Kirk McNulty
Understanding Manhood in America by Robert G. Davis
William Preston and His Work by Colin Dyer

WORKS CITED

Allegro, John M. *The Sacred Mushroom and the Cross: A study of the nature and origins of Christianity within the fertility cults of the ancient Near East.* Gnostic Media Research and Publishing. 2009

American Ethnology Bureau. *Annual Reports.* Government Printing Office, Washington. 1904

Barrett, Francis. *The Magus: A Complete System of Occult Philosophy.* Red Wheel/Weiser/Conari, Newburypory, MA. 2000

Bennett, Chris. *Cannabis and the Soma Solution.* TrineDay LLC, OR. 2010

Bennett, Chris. "Cannabis: The Philosopher's Stone." *Alchemy Lab Website.* http://www.alchemylab.com/cannabis_stone1.htm. Accessed Dec. 31, 2016

Blake, William. *The Marriage of Heaven and Hell.* Oxford University Press. 1975

Blavatsky, H.P. *The Secret Doctrine: The Synthesis of Science, Religion, and Philosophy.* Cambridge University Press. 2011

Bradshaw, Wesley. "George Washington's Vision." *The National Tribune*, vol. 4 no. 12, December, 1880

Britten, William. *Art Magic, or Mundane, Sub-Mundane and Super-Mundane Spiritism.* Progressive Thinker Publishing House, Chicago, IL. 1909

Brown, Robert Hewitt. *Stellar Theology and Masonic Astrology.* The Book Tree, San Diego, CA. 2002

Burton, Sir Richard Francis. *The City of the Saints: And Across the Rocky Mountains to California*. Harper and Brothers Publishers, NY. 1862

Campbell, Joseph. *The Hero with a Thousand Faces*. New World Library, Novato, California. 2008

Carpenter, Audrey T. *John Theophilus Desaguliers: A Natural Philosopher, Engineer, and Freemason in Newtonian England*. Continuum International Publishing Group, New York. 2011

Catlow, B.J. "Pub Med." *Effects of psilocybin on hippocampal neurogenesis and extinction of trace fear conditioning*. https://www.ncbi.nlm.nih.gov/m/pubmed/23727882/. Accessed Dec. 4, 2016

Cooke, Mordecai. *The Seven Sisters of Sleep*. Park Street Press, Rochester, Vermont. 1997

Cottonwood Research Foundation, Inc. *NEW: DMT Found in the Pineal Gland of Live Rats*. May 23, 2013. http://www.cottonwoodresearch.org/dmt-pineal-2013/. Accessed Dec. 5, 2016

Crowley, Aleister. *Book of the Law*. Weiser Books, NY. 1987

Crowley, Aleister. *The Blue Equinox: The Equinox, Volume III No. 1*. Weiser Books, NY. 2007

Crowley, Mike. "Oriental Jones and the Medal of Freedom." *Psychedelic American*, vol. 1, no. 1, 2015

Crowley, Mike. *Secret Drugs in Buddhism*. Amrita Press, CA. 2017

Davidson, Peter. *The Mistletoe and Its Philosophy*. Peter Davidson, Loudsville, White Co., GA., U.S.A. 1898

De Hoyos, Arturo. *Albert Pike's Masonic Formulas and Rituals*. The Supreme Council, 33°, Southern Jurisdiction, U.S.A. 2010

De Hoyos, Arturo. *Albert Pike's Morals and Dogma: Annotated Edition*. The Supreme Council, 33°, Southern Jurisdiction, U.S.A. 2011

De Hoyos, Arturo. *Scottish Rite Ritual Monitor and Guide*. The Supreme Council, 33°, Southern Jurisdiction, U.S.A. 2010

De Hoyos, Arturo. "The Melissino System of Freemasonry." *Collectanea* vol. 23 pt. 1. The Grand College of Rites of the U.S.A. 2014

De Hoyos, Arturo. "The Rite of Strict Observance and Two High Degree Rituals of the Eighteenth Century." *Collectanea* vol. 21 pt. 1. The Grand College of Rites, U.S.A. 2010

De Laurence, L.W. *The Hermetic and Alchemical Writings of Aureolus Phillippus Theophrastus Bombast of Hohenheim, Called Paracelsus, the Great by A.E. Waite*. De Laurence, Scott & Co., Chicago, IL. 1910

De Nerval, Gerard. *Journey to the Orient*. Peter Owen Publishers, London. 1972

Deveney, John Patrick. *Paschal Beverly Randolph: A Nineteenth Century Black American Spiritualist, Rosicrucian, and Sex Magician*. State University of New York Press. 1997

Dom, David. *King Arthur and the Gods of the Round Table*. Lulu.com. 2013

Eyer, Shawn. "Psychedelic Effects and the Eleusinian Mysteries." *Alexandria: The Journal of the Western Cosmological Traditions*, vol. 2. 1993

Faivre, Antoine. *The Golden Fleece and Alchemy*. State University of New York Press. 1993

Faulks, Philippa. *The Masonic Magician: The Life and Death of Count Cagliostro and His Egyptian Rite*. Watkins, London. 2008

Fietz, Lothar. *Aldous Huxley: Pratexte und Kontexte*. Lit Verlag, Munster. 2005

Fike, Matthew A. *The One Mind: C.G. Jung and the Future of Literary Criticism*. Routledge, London. 2014

Fleming, Nic. "BBC Earth." *Truffles contain 'bliss' molecule*. Dec. 18, 2014. http://www.bbc.com/earth/story/20141221-truffles-contain-bliss-molecule. Accessed Dec. 5, 2016

Ford, Gary. "The O.T.O. is Clandestine Masonry." *Phoney Masonry of the O.T.O.* http://blog.sina.com.cn/s/

Gardner, Martin. *The Annotated Alice*. W.W. Norton and Company, London. 2000

Ghose, Tia. "Live Science." *Magic Mushrooms Create a Hyperconnected Brain.* Oct. 29, 2014. http://www.livescience.com/48502-magic-mushrooms-change-brain-networks.html. Accessed Dec. 5, 2016

Gilbert, R.A. *The True and Perfect Preparation of the Philosopher's Stone, by the Brotherhood of the Order of the Golden and Rosy Cross*. Teitan Press, York Beach, Maine. 2013

Godwin, Joscelyn. *The Hermetic Brotherhood of Luxor: Initiatic and Historical Documents of an Order of Practical Occultism*. Samuel Weiser, Inc., York Beach, Maine. 1995

Grand College of Rites. "Fratres Lucis." *Collectanea* vol. 1 pt. 2. Grand College of Rites, U.S.A. 1978

Grand Lodge of Pennsylvania. *Proceedings of the Right Worshipful Freemasons of the Grand Lodge of Pennsylvania*. Grand Lodge of PA, Philadelphia. 1902

Greshko, Michael. "National Geographic." I*saac Newton's Lost Alchemy Recipe Rediscovered.* April 4, 2016. http://news.nationalgeographic.com/2016/04/160404-isaac-newton-alchemy-mercury-recipe-chemistry-science/. Accessed Nov. 11, 2016

Greswell, Edward. *Origines Kalendariae Hellenicae*. Oxford University Press. 1862

Guenon, Rene. *Studies in Freemasonry and the Compagnonnage*. Sophia Perenis, NY. 2004

Hamill, John. *The Rosicrucian Seer: Magical Writings of Frederick Hockley*. The Teitan Press, York Beach, Maine. 2009

Harms, Daniel. *The Book of Oberon: A Sourcebook of Elizabethan Magic*. Llewellyn Publications, MN. 2015

Harrison, David. "The Masonic Enlightenment: John Theophilus Desaguliers and the Birth of Modern Freemasonry." *Knight Templar Magazine*. http://www.knightstemplar.org/KnightTemplar/articles/enlightenment.htm. Accessed Dec. 13, 2016

Harrison, Jane Ellen. *Prolegomena to the Study of Greek Religion*. Princeton University Press, NJ. 1991

Heinrich, Clark. *Magic Mushrooms in Religion and Alchemy*. Park Street Press, Rochester, Vermont. 2002

Heinrich, Clark. *Strange Fruit: Alchemy and Religion, the Hidden Truth*. Bloomsbury, London. 1995

Hopkinson, N. *Callimachus' Hymn to Demeter*. Cambridge University Press. 2004

Howe, Ellic. "Grand Lodge of British Columbia and Yukon." *Fringe Masonry in England 1870-85*, Sept. 14, 1972. http://freemasonry.bcy.ca/aqc/fringe/fringe.html Accessed Dec. 4, 2016

Hughes, Michael M. "Michael M. Hughes: Writer, Speaker, Magical Thinker." *Sacred Intentions: Inside the Johns Hopkins Psilocybin Studies*. Oct. 8, 2008. http://michaelmhughes.com/sacred-intentions-inside-the-johns-hopkins-psilocybin-studies/. Accessed Dec. 10, 2016

Irwin, Herbert. *Book of Magic*. Society of Esoteric Endeavor. 2014

Jennings, Hargrave. *The Rosicrucians: Their Rites and Mysteries*. Cambridge University Press. 2011

J.H.O.M. (Jewish Heritage Online Magazine). "Stones." *A Magical Worm Called Shamir*. http://jhom.com/topics/stones/shamir.html. Accessed Dec. 7, 2016

Jung, C.G. *The Collected Works*. Routledge, NY. 2014

LaPort, Erik J. *Cracking the Philosopher's Stone*. Quintessence, Hanover Park, IL. 2015

WORKS CITED

LaPort, Erik J. *Keys to the Kingdom of Alchemy*. Quintessence, Hanover Park, IL. 2015

Levi, Eliphas. *Transcendental Magic: Its Doctrine and Ritual*. The Occult Publishing House, Chicago. 1910

Li, Xi-Wen. "*Cinnamonum Cassia.*" *Flora of China*. Missouri Botanical Garden, St. Louis, MO. http://www.efloras.org/florataxon.aspx?flora_id=2&taxon_id=200008698. Accessed Dec. 15, 2016

Libavius, Andreas. "The Alchemy Website." *Images of Alchemical Apparatus*. http://www.levity.com/alchemy/libav06.html. Accessed Dec. 6, 2016

L.I.G.H.T. (The Learning Institute for Growth, Healing and Transformation). "A Critical Appraisal." *Drugs, Alcohol and Food*. http://gaiancorps.com/study/psychology-mind/fourth-way/critical-appraisal/item/21-gurdjieff-%E2%80%93-drugs-alcohol-and-food?tmpl=component&print=1. Accessed Dec. 4, 2016

Mackey, Albert G. *A Lexicon of Freemasonry*. Richard Griffin and Company, London and Glasgow. 1860

Mackey, Albert G. "Phoenixmasonry." *Encyclopedia of Freemasonry and Its Kindred Sciences*. http://www.phoenixmasonry.org/mackeys_encyclopedia/a.htm. Accessed Dec. 6, 2016

Mackey, Albert G. *The Symbolism of Freemasonry*. Clark and Maynard, New York. 1869

Maier, Michael. *A Subtle Allegory: Concerning the Secrets of Alchemy*. CreateSpace Independent Publishing Platform. 2016

Maier, Michael. "The Alchemy Website." *Atalanta fugiens, emblems* 31-35. http://www.levity.com/alchemy/atl31-4.html. Accessed Dec. 6, 2016

Mathiesen, Robert. "The Unseen Worlds of Emma Hardinge Britten: Some Chapters in the History of Western Occultism." *Theosophical Occasional Papers*, vol. 9, 2001

Matt, Daniel Chanan. *Zohar, the Book of Enlightenment*. Paulist Press, NY. 1983

McIntosh, Christopher. *Eliphas Levi and the French Occult Revival.* State University of New York Press. 2011

McKenna, Terence. *Food of the Gods.* Bantam, New York. 1993

McKenna, Terence. *Psychedelia: Rap Dancing Into the 3rd Millenium.* Talk. Accessed: https://archive.org/

Mackenzie, Kenneth R.H. *The Royal Masonic Cyclopedia.* Harpercollins, Nashville, TN. 1987

Merkur, Dan. *The Mystery of Manna: The Psychedelic Sacrament of the Bible.* Park Street Press, Rochester Vermont. 2000

Metzner, Ralph. *Sacred Vine of Spirits: Ayahuasca.* Park Street Press, Rochester, Vermont. 2006

Meyer, Marvin W. *The Ancient Mysteries: A Sourcebook of Sacred Texts.* University of Pennsylvania Press, Philadelphia. 1999

Morris, S. Brent. "The Post Boy Sham Exposure of 1723." *Heredom*, vol. 7, 1998, pp. 9-38

Morris, Hamilton. "Vice." *Hamilton and the Philosopher's Stone.* http://www.vice.com/video/hamilton-and-the-philosophers-stone-part-1. Accessed Dec. 5, 2016

Naturalpedia. *Quotes about apathy from the world's top natural health/natural living authors.* http://www.naturalpedia.com/Apathy-5.html. Accessed Dec. 7, 2016

Oss, O.T. *Psilocybin Mushroom Grower's Guide.* Quick American Archives, San Francisco. 1993

Ott, Jonathan. *Pharmacotheon.* Natural Products Company, WA. 1996

Pedley, Les. "Another View of *Racosperma.*" *Acacia study group newsletter* (90): 3. http://worldwidewattle.com/socgroups/asg/newsletters/90.pdf. Accessed Dec. 15, 2016

Picknett, Lynn. *The Templar Revelation: Secret Guardians of the True Identity of*

Christ. Touchstone, NY. 1997

Pike, Albert. *Legenda of the Lodge of Perfection*. The Supreme Council, 33°, Southern Jurisdiction, Charleston. 1888

Pike, Albert. *The Book of the Words*. The Scottish Rite Research Society, Washington, D.C. 1999

Plattard, Jean. *The Life of Francois Rebelais*. Frank Cass & Co. LTD. 1968

Propaganda Anonymous. "The Fatimiya Sufi Order and Ayahuasca." *Reality Sandwich*. http://realitysandwich.com/76773/fatimiya_sufi_ayahuasca/. Accessed Dec. 31, 2016

Regardie, Israel. *777 and Other Qabalistic Writings of Aleister Crowley*. Weiser Books, Boston, MA. 1977

Ratsch, Christian. *The Encyclopedia of Psychoactive Plants: Ethnopharmacology and Its Applications*. Park Street Press, Rochester, Vermont. 2005

Ruck, Carl A.P. *Mushrooms, Myth and Mithras: The Drug Cult that Civilized Europe*. City Light Books, San Francisco. 2011

Ruck, Carl A.P. *Sacred Mushrooms of the Goddess and the Secrets of Eleusis*. Ronin Publishing, Inc., Berkeley, CA. 2006

Ruck, Carl A.P. *The Apples of Apollo: Pagan and Christian Mysteries of the Eucharist*. Carolina Academic Press, Durham, NC. 2001

Rudgley, Richard. *The Encyclopedia of Psychoactive Substances*. St. Martin's Press, NY. 1999

Ryall, Julian. "National Geographic." *Lightning Makes Mushrooms Multiply*. April 10, 2010. http://news.nationalgeographic.com/news/2010/04/100409-lightning-mushrooms-japan-harvest/. Accessed Dec. 7, 2016

Sabazius X°. *Essays, Notes, and Speeches*. http://lib.oto-usa.org/wp/essays/sabazius-x/. Accessed Dec. 7, 2016

Shade, Frederick, A. "Knight Templar Magazine." *The Quest for the Holy Grail and the Modern Knights Templar*. http://www.knighttemplar.org/KnightTemplar/articles/20111021.htm. Accessed Dec. 7, 2016

Shah, Idris. *The Sufis*. ISF Publishing, Richardson, TX. 2015

Shanon, Benny. "Biblical Entheogens: A Speculative Hypothesis." *Time and Mind: The Journal of Archaeology, Consciousness, and Culture*, vol. 1 – issue 1, March, 2008, pp. 51-74

Sorabji, Richard. *Animal Minds and Human Morals: The Origins of the Western Debate*. Cornell University Press, NY. 1993

S.R.I.C.F. *First Order Ritual*. Societas Rosicruciana In Civitatibus Foederatis. U.S.A. 2007

Starr, Martin P. "Aleister Crowley: Freemason!" *Grand Lodge of British Columbia and Yukon*. http://freemasonry.bcy.ca/aqc/crowley.html. Accessed Dec. 14, 2016

Stavish, Mark. *The History of Alchemy in America*, 1996. http://hermetic.com/stavish/alchemy/history.html. Accessed Dec. 5, 2016

Strassman, Rick. *DMT: The Spirit Molecule: A Doctor's Revolutionary Research into the Biology of Near-Death and Mystical Experiences*. Park Street Press, Rochester, Vermont. 2001

Taylor, Joan E. *The Essenes, the Scrolls, and the Dead Sea*. Oxford University Press. 2012

The Hermetic Library Blog. *Thelema Coast to Coast*, #4, May 14, 2005. http://library.hrmtc.com/tag/tony-stansfeld-jones/. Accessed Dec. 7, 2016

The Holy Bible. Authorized King James Version. Master Mason Edition. Heirloom Bible Publishers, Wichita, Kansas. 1991

The Telegraph. *Dr. Humphry Osmond*. Feb. 26, 2004. http://www.telegraph.co.uk/news/obituaries/1454436/Dr-Humphry-Osmond.html Accessed Dec. 7, 2016

Torres, Constantino Manuel. *Anadenanthera: Visionary Plant of Ancient South America*. The Haworth Herbal Press. NY, London, Oxford. 2006

TravellersGarden.com. *Oliloqui*. http://www.travellersgarden.com/product-info.php?category=5&subcategory=0&productmain=1043. Accessed Dec. 7, 2016

TV Tropes. *Bill Hicks (Creator)*. http://tvtropes.org/pmwiki/pmwiki.php/Creator/BillHicks. Accessed Dec. 10, 2016

Twyman, Tracy R. "Tracy R. Twyman." *Found Again: The "Templar Artifacts" of Hammer-Purgstall*. http://tracytwyman.com/found-again-the-templar-artifacts-of-hammer-purgstall/. Accessed Dec. 7, 2016

U.D., Frater. *High Magic II: Expanded Theory and Practice*. Llewellyn Worldwide, Woodbury, MN. 2005

Vivekananda, Swami. *Raja Yoga*. Brentano's, NY. 1920

Waite, Arthur Edward. *The History of Magic by Eliphas Levi*. Weiser Books, Boston, MA/York Beach, ME. 2003

Waite, Arthur Edward. *The Mysteries of Magic: A Digest of the Writings of Eliphas Levi*. George Redway, York Street, Covent Garden, London. 1886

Ward, J.S.M. *Freemasonry and the Ancient Gods*. Simpkin, Marshall, Hamilton, and Kent, London. 1921

Wasson, R. Gordon. *Persephone's Quest: Entheogens and the Origins of Religion*. Yale University Press, New Haven and London. 1986

Wasson, R. Gordon. "Seeking the Magic Mushroom." *LIFE Magazine*, June 10, 1957

Wasson, R. Gordon. *Soma: Divine Mushroom of Immortality*. Harcourt Brace Jovanovich, San Diego. 1972

Wasson, R. Gordon. *The Road to Eleusis: Unveiling the Secret of the Mysteries*. North Atlantic Books. 2008

Weeks, Andrew. *Paracelsus (Theophrastus Bombastus Von Hohenheim, 1493-*

1541): Essential Theoretical Writings. Brill, Leiden, Boston. 2008

Weidner, Jay. *The Mysteries of the Great Cross of Hendaye.* Destiny Books, Rochester, Vermont. 2003

Wilmshurst, W.L. *The Meaning of Masonry.* William Rider and Son. 1922

Wright, Ichabod Wright. *The Inferno of Dante.* Longman, Rees, Orme, Brown, Green, and Longman, Nottingham. 1833

Yarker, John. *The Arcane Schools.* Cosimo Classics, NY. 2007

Yarker, John. "The Society of the Rose Cross." *The Rosicrucian Brotherhood*, vol. 1, no. 3, July, 1907, pp. 113-24

Yates, Frances A. *The Rosicrucian Enlightenment.* Routledge Classics, London and New York. 2002

WORKS CITED

Printed in Great Britain
by Amazon